W9-BVO-002

3 5674 02187494 7

Pl   ns

KN

Plays of
Black Americans

*Episodes from the black experience
in America, dramatized
for young people*

Edited by SYLVIA E. KAMERMAN

Publishers   PLAYS, INC.   *Boston*

Library of Congress Cataloging-in-Publication Data

Plays of Black Americans.

Summary: This collection of plays focusing on the Black experience in America includes "The Hall of Black American Heroes," "John Henry," I Have a Dream," and eight others.
1. Afro-Americans—Juvenile drama. 2. American drama—Afro-American authors. 3. Children's plays, American. [1. Afro-Americans—Drama. 2. Plays— Collections] I. Kamerman, Sylvia E.
PS627.N4P55 1987 812'.54'0803520396073 87-12207
ISBN 0-8238-0279-5 (pbk.)

Contents

Plays of Black Americans

The Hall of Black American Heroes

by Mary Satchell

Characters

GUIDE
MISS WILLIAMS, *teacher*
NATALIE ⎤
MIKE ⎟
GARY ⎟
JOAN ⎬ *students*
SYLVIA ⎟
J. C. ⎦

CRISPUS ATTUCKS ⎤
SOJOURNER TRUTH ⎟
HARRIET TUBMAN ⎟ *Black*
FREDERICK DOUGLASS ⎬ *American*
JACKIE ROBINSON ⎟ *heroes*
WILMA RUDOLPH ⎟
SUGAR RAY LEONARD ⎦

JOHN MILLER ⎤
HENRY JENKINS ⎟
TUBMAN'S MOTHER ⎟ *extras*
MATRON ⎬
DOCTOR ⎟
TWO BOXERS ⎦

3

TIME: *The present.*

SETTING: *A small exhibition hall. Up center are seven large bust portraits arranged in a semi-circle facing audience. The portraits, from right to left, represent Crispus Attucks, Sojourner Truth, Harriet Tubman, Frederick Douglass, Jackie Robinson, Wilma Rudolph, Sugar Ray Leonard. Name plates with dates are below each portrait. Banner above reads:* HALL OF BLACK AMERICAN HEROES. *Velvet cord, in front of portraits, stretches across stage, as a protective barrier. Chair and small desk with pamphlets, writing paper, quill pen, and inkwell are down right. Small wastebasket is beside exit at left. There is also exit right.*

AT RISE: GUIDE *enters right, turns and calls off right.*

GUIDE: Right this way, please. This is the next stop of our museum tour. *(With enthusiasm)* Welcome to the Hall of Black American Heroes! (GUIDE *steps aside to make way for* MISS WILLIAMS, NATALIE, MIKE, GARY, JOAN, SYLVIA *and* J.C., *who enter. All look bored, except* JOAN, *who holds notepad and pencil and walks behind* MISS WILLIAMS. GARY *carries radio.* J.C. *has comic book in his back pocket.* GUIDE *points to portraits.)* The first four portraits here represent some of our most famous black Americans who were born slaves, and dedicated their lives to the cause of freedom. The last three portraits are sports heroes who may be very familiar to you. (JOAN *takes notes. Others whisper to each other or fidget.)*

MISS WILLIAMS *(Eagerly):* Pay attention! This is the highlight of our visit to the museum today.

NATALIE: I don't see anything to be excited about, Miss Williams.

MIKE: You're right, Natalie. This place is too quiet.

(Grimaces) It gives me the creeps. *(To* MISS WILLIAMS*)* Why couldn't we have gone to a really exciting place like Sunnyland Park?

GARY: Or the skating rink. They have the best disco music in town.

MISS WILLIAMS *(Sternly)*: Gary and Mike. Pay attention. This tour is the best way to prepare for the exam next week. *(Students groan.)*

JOAN *(Eagerly)*: Exam? I'd better get busy. *(Moves quickly to a portrait and jots down name and dates)*

SYLVIA *(Sullenly)*: I knew there had to be a catch to this field trip.

GUIDE *(Pleasantly)*: I think you'll like these heroes once you get to know them.

NATALIE *(Defiantly)*: Why do you call them heroes? A hero is someone who's done something great.

GARY *(Facing* ATTUCKS*)*: He doesn't look too heroic to me.

GUIDE *(Moving to* ATTUCKS' *portrait)*: But that's not so. Crispus Attucks was one of the first persons to die for America's freedom. *(Moves to* TRUTH*)* Sojourner Truth was born a slave in New York. She was named Isabella at birth, but she later called herself Sojourner Truth. She traveled the country, preaching freedom. *(Stands near* TUBMAN*)* Harriet Tubman was called the Moses of our people. Harriet was born into slavery and later escaped to freedom. She led her parents and hundreds of other slaves to free soil. *(Points to* DOUGLASS*)* Frederick Douglass chose to put his life in jeopardy rather than live as a free man in England. *(While* GUIDE *is talking, students' attention wanders.* SYLVIA *opens her purse and rummages inside;* MIKE *looks around aimlessly;* NATALIE *yawns;* GARY *eyes items on desk; J.C. stands behind* GARY *and peeks at* *his magazine;* JOAN *scribbles constantly on notepad.*)

MISS WILLIAMS *(Enthusiastically; turning to class):* This is all so interesting! (SYLVIA *has taken out lipstick and begins to apply it.*) Sylvia, put that lipstick away.

SYLVIA *(Protesting):* But, Miss Williams, I hate history.

MISS WILLIAMS *(Admonishing):* Sylvia. (SYLVIA *sighs and reluctantly puts lipstick away.*)

GUIDE *(A bit hurried):* I think we'd better hurry along. *(Points to desk)* Those pamphlets give brief accounts of each hero's life.

GARY *(Walking toward desk):* I'll get the pamphlets for you. (MISS WILLIAMS *sees* J.C.)

MISS WILLIAMS: J.C. Anderson! (J.C. *looks up, startled.*) Throw that magazine away and pay attention! (J.C. *goes, muttering, to wastebasket and drops magazine in; he puts hands in pockets and sulks.*)

JOAN *(Sympathetically):* Our field trip doesn't seem to be going very well. (GARY *passes out pamphlets.*)

GUIDE *(Optimistically):* There *is* another way to get through this tour. *(Moves downstage)* Let's allow all of our heroes to tell their own stories. You and I will watch as history unfolds before our eyes.

JOAN *(Curiously):* How can we do that?

GUIDE: Just let your thoughts wander back through the halls of time. As we follow our heroes during important moments in their lives, we'll see some suffering and pain, but there will be much faith, hope, and joy. These black Americans were not born great, but they became heroes because they were determined to face life courageously. *(Lights fade. Students,* GUIDE, *and* MISS WILLIAMS *exit. When lights come up again, real characters have replaced portraits.* CRISPUS ATTUCKS *stands beside* HARRIET TUBMAN, *who holds unlit candle.* SOJOURNER TRUTH *sits on bench down left.*

FREDERICK DOUGLASS *stands pensive with hands behind him.* JACKIE ROBINSON *stands holding bat against shoulder.* WILMA RUDOLPH *sits in chair.* SUGAR RAY LEONARD *stands to her left. All remain still, then make small, natural movements, relaxing at same time.)*

CRISPUS ATTUCKS *(Proudly):* I, Crispus Attucks, was one of the first persons to die for this country. That was many years ago, and I was young then . . . full of life and eager to live it. *(Moves down center; light fades to only a spotlight on* ATTUCKS) Was I afraid to die? I had no thought of dying. The young think they will live forever. *(Pausing)* I'll never forget my last day here in 1770. My friend John Miller and I were talking about the sad state of affairs in our beloved Boston. *(*JOHN MILLER *enters spotlight.)*

JOHN MILLER: This city's going to explode any day now.

CRISPUS ATTUCKS *(Confidently):* Boston will hold out no matter how many hardships England may put on us.

JOHN MILLER *(Glancing furtively over his shoulder):* There are many rumors abroad. People say that Sam Adams and his Sons of Liberty are planning a rebellion against the British soldiers.

CRISPUS ATTUCKS *(Interested):* Aye, I'd welcome the chance to join that rebellion. These Redcoats watch our every move. They're scaring our citizens, breaking down doors and searching houses. *(*HENRY JENKINS *enters, stands outside spotlight.)*

JOHN MILLER *(Putting hand to ear and peering into darkness):* Who goes there?

HENRY JENKINS *(From darkness; cautiously):* Henry Jenkins. *(Steps into spotlight; urgently)* I've been looking all over for you two.

CRISPUS ATTUCKS: What's wrong?

HENRY JENKINS: There's trouble at the Custom House. The British guard on duty hit a man on the head with the butt of his gun.

CRISPUS ATTUCKS (Angrily): It's time for us to act! We can't endure these wrongs any longer.

JOHN MILLER: Let's join the Sons of Liberty.

HENRY JENKINS (Excitedly): There's no time for that. That situation's already getting out of hand.

JOHN MILLER: We'll need a leader; someone who can rally the others.

HENRY JENKINS: Someone willing to put his life on the line. Those Redcoats are heavily armed, and we have only sticks and stones.

JOHN MILLER: A man would be out of his mind to take on a task like that.

CRISPUS ATTUCKS (Quickly): I'll do it. (Others look intently at ATTUCKS.) They'll listen to me. I've made no secret about my feelings.

JOHN MILLER (Soberly): Attucks, we're behind you.

HENRY JENKINS: Yes!

CRISPUS ATTUCKS (Urgently): Then, let's go. There is no time to lose. I'll lead the way to King Street. (Moving to left) We must round up as many men as we can. (Strides resolutely out of spotlight; others follow quickly and exit. Spotlight goes out; ATTUCKS takes place as portrait again, and GUIDE and NATALIE enter and stand in front of him. Spotlight goes up on them.)

GUIDE: Crispus Attucks died in the Boston Massacre.

NATALIE (Surprised): I didn't know one of the first men to die fighting the British was a black man. (Light goes out. NATALIE and GUIDE exit. Spotlight up on SOJOURNER TRUTH, sitting, hunched, on bench.)

SOJOURNER TRUTH (Morosely): I was called Isabella

when I was born a slave in 1797. *(Proudly)* But the Lord gave me a new name—Sojourner Truth. He told me to go forth and take throughout this land His message of freedom from slavery and injustice, and that's what I must do. *(Stands facing audience)* It's cold and rainy tonight, and I'm weary. I've traveled for many miles across this country, in the cold and heat; most of the time alone, without friend or companion. Many people hate me, fear the words I have to say. Some of them laugh, and say I'm out of my mind. The things I talk about make no sense to them. *(Nods)* That's what they say. But I know that, in every human heart, there beats the same rhythm—a desperate, crying need to be free. *(Brooding a moment)* I've been beaten in some towns, and run out of others. Yet, it makes no difference. I must go on. *(With fervor)* I have a mission to walk this great land, and tell the truth to all who will hear. *(Raising hands high over head)* I bring the truth message of freedom! (*Lights go out quickly; J.C. and* MIKE *enter, left. When lights go up, they are peering at pamphlet.*)

MIKE *(Admiringly):* I don't know if I would have risked my life traveling all over the country like that.

J.C.: It took real courage for Sojourner Truth to keep going the way she did, year after year. (*Lights go out. J.C. and* MIKE *exit. Spotlight comes up on* HARRIET TUBMAN, *up center. She lights candle and holds near face.*)

HARRIET TUBMAN *(To audience):* I am Harriet Tubman, and this is my light of freedom. I keep it beside me, always. I hope my light has guided the footsteps of many Americans born after I passed this way. *(She blows out candle.)* It was this light of freedom that led me to plan my escape from the bonds of slavery in

1849. I followed that light North, where I thought happiness was waiting. But my heart led me back to my parents in Maryland. They had never known the joy of freedom. *(Pauses)* I remember our escape to New York in 1857 as if it happened only yesterday. I had vowed to lead my mother and father away to a new life. (MOTHER *enters, sits on bench. Light goes up on her.* TUBMAN *looks toward* MOTHER.) There's Mother waiting for me now. It makes my heart ache to see her looking so frail, and knowing we have such a long journey ahead of us. *(Light on* MOTHER *fades.)*

MOTHER *(From dimness):* Is that you, my child?

HARRIET TUBMAN *(Moving downstage, with spotlight following her):* Yes, Mother. *(Puts candle on bench, takes off shawl and gently places it around* MOTHER's *shoulders)* It's cold and damp in this cellar, Mother.

MOTHER: I don't mind the cold, Harriet. My old heart feels warm every time I think about what lies ahead.

HARRIET TUBMAN *(Intensely):* I've dreamed of this day ever since I escaped to Philadelphia, years ago. Freedom. Freedom for you and Father, who never knew anything but the yoke of slavery since the day you were born.

MOTHER: You're risking your life to rescue us. *(Earnestly)* I've worried about you. Risking your life, time after time, to lead other slaves to freedom—there's a bounty on your head.

HARRIET TUBMAN: Don't be afraid, Mother. We have many friends to help us along the way.

MOTHER *(Looking about curiously):* Whose house is this we're hiding in?

HARRIET TUBMAN: Thomas Garrett, a Quaker. He's helped many of my friends before.

MOTHER: Is your father still asleep?

HARRIET TUBMAN *(Sighing):* Yes, he's worn out. You should be getting some rest, too. We'll be heading for the next station well after midnight.

MOTHER: I'm too excited to sleep.

HARRIET TUBMAN: We have a long, long way to go before you're safe. *(Pausing)* Mother, do you know what I did when I first crossed the line between slavery and freedom? *(Holding hands up)* I looked at my hands. I wanted to be sure that I was the same person once I was free. *(Joyfully)* The sun was shining like gold through the trees and across the fields!

MOTHER: Then why did you come back here?

HARRIET TUBMAN *(Solemnly):* Because I was lonely. I was free, but I was in a land of strangers, and all my loved ones were still back here. I promised myself to make a home for all of you, to take you to freedom. *(Lifting head; triumphantly)* And, I have kept my vow. *(Kneeling beside* MOTHER*)* I kept my vow! *(Spotlight on* TUBMAN *and* MOTHER *goes out;* GUIDE *and* GARY *enter. Spotlight goes up on them.)*

GARY: Did Harriet Tubman make it safely to freedom with her parents?

GUIDE: Yes, Gary. They arrived in New York in 1857.

GARY *(Thoughtfully):* I think I'll find out more about Harriet Tubman's life. She was quite a lady! *(*JOAN *enters and stands beside* GARY *and* GUIDE *as spotlight goes up on* FREDERICK DOUGLASS, *waiting at desk, down right.)*

JOAN *(To* GUIDE*):* What did Frederick Douglass do?

GUIDE: Frederick Douglass was a very courageous man. He was a fugitive slave who never stopped fighting for the rights of black people, and even risked his freedom and his life by publishing an autobiography in 1845. *(Light goes out on* GUIDE, JOAN, *and* GARY. MATRON *walks briskly into spotlight. She carries a book.*)

MATRON: Mr. Douglass, would you be kind enough to autograph your new book for me?

FREDERICK DOUGLASS (*Standing and bowing courteously*): With pleasure, madam. *(Taking book)* You and your countrymen have been very kind to me during my stay here in England. *(Signing with quill and returning book)*

MATRON: Mr. Douglass, you are one of the most famous men in the world. England would be glad to have you make this country your permanent home.

FREDERICK DOUGLASS: I appreciate your sentiment, but my real home is America. No matter what problems it may have, I still have great faith in my country.

MATRON: I've never been to America, yet I'm saddened by the state of affairs there. My husband believes your country is on the brink of a civil war.

FREDERICK DOUGLASS (*Gravely*): I wish I could say he's wrong, but I cannot. *(Pauses)* I'll be leaving for home in a few weeks—as soon as my lecture tour is over.

MATRON (*Shocked*): Leaving for America! But that's like committing yourself to prison, Mr. Douglass. You've told the world in your book that you're a runaway slave. Do you know what will happen when you return?

FREDERICK DOUGLASS (*Resigned*): I know all too well, but I must go.

MATRON (*In awe*): You would turn your back on all that England can give you—admiration, comfort, and financial security?

FREDERICK DOUGLASS: I've been tempted to take that easy road and stay in England, but my country needs me, and I need my country. I must help in the struggle against slavery because I can never know happiness, I can never know security, I can *never* be free till my people are free.

MATRON: I am beginning to understand what a truly great man you are, Mr. Douglass. I hope your country will appreciate the sacrifice you're making. (DOUGLASS *takes* MATRON's *arm and they exit. Lights come up on* JACKIE ROBINSON, WILMA RUDOLPH, *and* SUGAR RAY LEONARD. SYLVIA *and* MISS WILLIAMS *enter and pause before portraits.*)

SYLVIA *(Casually):* But Jackie Robinson, Wilma Rudolph, and Sugar Ray Leonard are sports heroes. They were never slaves.

MISS WILLIAMS: That's true, Sylvia. These sports figures as well as the rest of us have many black American pioneers to thank for that.

SYLVIA: Jackie Robinson was the first black man to play Major League baseball. Did he have to struggle for equality?

MISS WILLIAMS *(Thinking):* Let's see, Sylvia. (*Lights go out.* MISS WILLIAMS *and* SYLVIA *exit. Spotlight goes up on* JACKIE ROBINSON, *who holds bat.*)

JACKIE ROBINSON *(Seriously):* They said I couldn't do it, that it wouldn't work. There had never been a black baseball player in the major leagues. Now, in 1947, I'd been brought up from the Montreal Royals, to play ball with one of the greatest major league teams of all time—the Brooklyn Dodgers. What a day that was for me! I was called into the manager's office and told the hard facts. There would be no bands playing or welcoming ceremonies when I walked onto that baseball field. I would face the greatest challenge of my life. There would be hundreds, even thousands of fans who wouldn't like to see me playing with the team, simply because I was black. *(Shakes head slowly)* Those first games were rough. Sometimes, I felt so alone out there on the field. *(Strongly)* Do you know what I did then? I'd think about the many black American pioneers who conquered their fears and achieved great heights. *(Triumphantly)* At the end of that first season with the Dodgers, I was voted Rookie of the Year, and my team won the pennant. *(Smiles)* I proved that it could be done! *(Exits left, from spotlight.* GUIDE, *followed by* NATALIE, SYLVIA, *and* JOAN, *enters right.)*

NATALIE *(To* GUIDE): These sports heroes are very different from the other heroes.

GUIDE: You'll find they aren't so different, Natalie, when you learn more about their lives. All of them have the same traits—strength, courage, and faith in themselves.

SYLVIA: I recognized the portraits of Jackie Robinson, the baseball player, and Sugar Ray Leonard, the boxer.

JOAN: So did I, Sylvia, but *(To* GUIDE) who was Wilma Rudolph?

GUIDE: Wilma Rudolph was once the fastest woman runner in the world. She won three Olympic gold medals in 1960, but she had to overcome a severe handicap before she became a champion track star. There was a time in her youth when everyone thought she'd never run at all. *(Spotlight moves to* WIILMA RUDOLPH, *who sits on bench, leaning forward.* DOCTOR *enters spotlight.)*

DOCTOR: What are you looking at, Wilma?

WILMA RUDOLPH *(With longing):* My friends are playing ball in the street, Doctor.

DOCTOR: You wish you could be out there with them, don't you?

WILMA RUDOLPH *(Smiling):* Oh, I *will* be out there with my friends someday.

DOCTOR *(Gently):* Wilma, it's nice to dream, but sometimes we have to face reality.

WILMA RUDOLPH *(Looking intently at* DOCTOR): What do you mean, Doctor?

DOCTOR *(Hesitantly):* Even though your scarlet fever didn't leave you permanently paralyzed, you'll have to be careful with your leg.

WILMA RUDOLPH: But, Doctor, I won't always have to walk with a limp. My mother says you're the best doctor in Tennessee, and I just know my leg will get well. *(Determined)* And then, I'll walk better than any of my friends. I'll run faster than everybody, one day— *you'll* see.

DOCTOR *(Thoughtfully):* It wouldn't surprise me if you did just that, Wilma. *(Spotlight moves to* BOXERS, *who are sparring with each other.* SUGAR RAY LEONARD *enters spotlight.)*

SUGAR RAY LEONARD *(Jokingly):* Looks as if you two need a referee. (BOXERS *stop and turn in surprise.)*

2ND BOXER *(Ad lib):* Sugar Ray Leonard!

1ST BOXER: What are you doing here?

SUGAR RAY LEONARD: I've been invited to speak to your club today.

2ND BOXER: I thought you'd be too busy to go around making speeches, Champ.

1ST BOXER: Isn't that dull after winning all those boxing titles?

SUGAR RAY LEONARD *(Seriously):* Talking to kids like you at schools and community clubs is a very important part of my life. I owe a lot to boxing, and to the many people who helped me get where I am.

2ND BOXER: You mean your parents and family?

SUGAR RAY LEONARD *(Nodding):* Parents, family, *and* friends. I also owe my thanks to many of the black American pioneers, people like Crispus Attucks, Sojourner Truth, Harriet Tubman, and Frederick Douglass. They made it possible for you and me to have the freedom to strive for our goals in life.

1ST BOXER: So you're saying that those black American pioneers are really heroes.

2ND BOXER: Just like you, Champ!

SUGAR RAY LEONARD *(Smiling):* They're heroes because they've done some truly great things.

2ND BOXER *(Jabbing at air):* I'm going to be a boxing champ someday.

1ST BOXER: *I'm* going to win the Olympic boxing gold medal, Champ, just as you did in 1976.

SUGAR RAY LEONARD *(Enthusiastically):* You two have a lot of hard work ahead, so let's get busy. (BOXERS *start sparring again, and* LEONARD *stands alert as referee. Lights go out;* SUGAR RAY LEONARD *and* BOXERS *exit. Lights come up.* GUIDE *stands center stage with* MISS WILLIAMS *and* STUDENTS.)

GUIDE: Well, that ends our tour of the Hall of Black American Heroes. I hope you didn't find it boring.

NATALIE: Boring! I haven't learned so many interesting things in a long time.

SYLVIA: And I never knew that history could be exciting!

MIKE: This tour can't beat the amusement park, but I'm glad we came here today, Miss Williams. Now I know how much these black Americans endured to be free.

J.C.: I agree. And this tour helped me understand that we owe *our* freedom to many courageous black Americans.

GARY: I've got a new respect for these men and women, especially the pioneers who lived during slavery.

JOAN *(Frantically scribbling on notepad):* And *I've* got a headache from trying to keep up with all of this! *(Others laugh.)*

MISS WILLIAMS: Don't worry, Joan. I think all of you have made A's today. You've passed my test with flying colors, and I'm proud of you. *(Students clap hands happily.)*

GUIDE: Goodbye, Miss Williams. I hope you all come back soon.

MISS WILLIAMS *(Cheerfully):* Thank you for a wonderful tour. I'll bring all of my classes back—often. (GUIDE *leads* MISS WILLIAMS *and class off, right. J.C. pauses, turns, moves to wastebasket to retrieve comic book, pockets it, then salutes portraits before rushing off, right. Curtain)*

THE END

PRODUCTION NOTES

THE HALL OF BLACK AMERICAN HEROES

Characters: 12 male; 10 female.

Playing Time: 30 minutes.

Costumes: Guide wears uniform. Attucks, Miller, and Jenkins have trousers and work shirts with sleeves rolled to elbow. Truth, Tubman, and Mother wear long dresses; Truth has on long apron and head scarf. Tubman carries candle and match; also has shawl. Douglass is in dark suit with long coat and stand-up collar; hair is greying. Matron wears long cape. Robinson wears baseball uniform and holds bat. Rudolph is in printed dress. Doctor carries satchel. Leonard is dressed in suit with tie. Boxers wear shorts, protective helmets, and boxing gloves. Students wear everyday clothes.

Properties: Notepad, pencil, comic book, radio, purse, lipstick, compact, candle, match, shawl, book.

Setting: A small exhibition hall. Up center, seven large bust portraits are arranged in a semi-circle facing audience. The portraits, from right to left, represent Crispus Attucks (c. 1723–1770), Sojourner Truth (c. 1797–1883), Harriet Tubman (c. 1820–1913), Frederick Douglass (c. 1817–1895), Jackie Robinson (1919–1972), Wilma Rudolph (1940–), Sugar Ray Leonard (1956–). Name plates with dates are below each portrait. Banner above portraits reads: HALL OF BLACK AMERICAN HEROES. A long cord, in front of portraits, stretches across stage as a protective barrier. A chair and small desk with pamphlets, writing paper, quill pen, and inkwell are down right. A small wastebasket is beside exit at left. Another exit is right.

Lighting: Spotlights; stage lights fading from bright to dark, as indicated in text. NOTE: Lighting is very important for creating atmosphere and providing desired effects.

George Washington Carver

by Mildred Hark and Noel McQueen

Characters

GEORGE, *George Washington Carver as a boy*
AUNT SUE CARVER
UNCLE MOSE CARVER
MARTHA
GEORGE WASHINGTON CARVER
PROFESSOR JAMES G. WILSON
SECRETARY
TWO REPORTERS
YOUNG MAN

SCENE 1

TIME: *The early 1870's.*

SETTING: *Interior of log house. There is a door up center and a window in left wall. At right is rough fireplace with cooking utensils hanging near it and rough mantel above it. There are pieces of pewter and roll of knitting on mantel. Two wooden beds are against upstage wall, on either side of door, and table is at center. Around table are two or three stools. Spinning wheel and stool stand downstage.*

19

AT RISE: AUNT SUE CARVER, *a middle-aged white woman, sits at spinning wheel, spinning. Door opens, and* GEORGE, *a small black boy of about ten, appears in doorway carrying a basket filled with plants, grasses, and flowers. He wears a wildflower in the buttonhole of his shirt.*

GEORGE *(Excitedly):* Aunt Sue!

AUNT SUE: George, where have you been? Uncle Mose is angry. He's been looking for you all morning.

GEORGE: I—I'm sorry, Aunt Sue. I didn't know I was gone long. I went to the woods.

AUNT SUE: Well, don't come inside with your rubbish.

GEORGE: But it isn't rubbish, Aunt Sue. I've found the most wonderful new bug!

AUNT SUE *(Sarcastically):* Bugs—wonderful. A bug is a bug.

GEORGE: And some kind of grass I've never seen before and a beautiful wildflower. *(Points to buttonhole)* See—I've got it in my buttonhole.

AUNT SUE *(Softening):* The flowers you bring back *are* beautiful. Those wild ones you've planted in the yard— the neighbors all say how lucky I am to have such a fine garden.

GEORGE: But if only I know the names of the flowers and what to call the bugs and what makes the different colors—

AUNT SUE: Questions, questions! Do you never get tired of asking questions? George, you should be going to school.

GEORGE: I have learned some from the speller you gave me.

AUNT SUE: But it isn't enough. You cannot learn the names of your bugs or your flowers from the speller—

you need to learn other things. Now, you'd better take your plants outside. Uncle Mose needs you.

GEORGE: But I wanted to show you what I have in the basket.

AUNT SUE *(Smiling):* All right. (*She puts her work down and gets up.* GEORGE *shuts door and comes downstage toward her.*) You ought to rest a bit after that long, hot walk to the woods, anyway. (GEORGE *takes plant out of basket and holds it up.*)

GEORGE: Look at this, Aunt Sue.

AUNT SUE *(Taking it):* What is this you've dug up so carefully? A weed?

GEORGE *(Taking it away from her):* No—no! It's a plant. It grows, so it must be good for something. I want to know what—

AUNT SUE: Want to know—want to know. I never saw such a child.

GEORGE: I wonder about everything, Aunt Sue. The other day, when I was in the woods, it started to rain, so I sat under a tree and the little ones sat with me.

AUNT SUE *(Puzzled):* Little ones? I suppose you mean the animals.

GEORGE: Yes! A rabbit, two squirrels, and a chipmunk. We all just sat there and waited until the rain stopped. And then there was a bright rainbow, and I started wondering about that. The colors were just like the colors in the flowers. You know, Aunt Sue, all those colors must be in the earth.

AUNT SUE: Why do you say that, George?

GEORGE: Well, the flowers grow right up out of the earth. The colors must come from somewhere.

AUNT SUE *(Affectionately):* If anyone ever finds them, you will.

GEORGE: And we can use those colors, Aunt Sue—look at this! *(He takes a flat stone from basket.)*

AUNT SUE *(As she examines it closely):* You've painted a picture on a stone! Where did you get the paint?

GEORGE: I made it from pikeberries, and I made a little brush from horse hair.

AUNT SUE: Where did you get the idea of painting pictures?

GEORGE: The other day, when Uncle Mose sent me to Farmer Baynham's on an errand, Mrs. Baynham took me in to look at her plants and showed me some pictures hanging on the walls in the parlor.

AUNT SUE *(Smiling):* So you had to try your hand at the same thing.

GEORGE: Well, while I was looking at them, I thought, "I can do that!" *(Matter of factly)* and I did. *(There is a knock on door.)*

AUNT SUE: George, will you put your things outside and see who that is?

GEORGE: Yes, Aunt Sue. *(He opens door for* MARTHA, *who carries package tied with string.)*

GEORGE: Oh, hello.

AUNT SUE *(Crossing to door):* Why, Martha, how nice of you to come by. Come in!

MARTHA *(Entering):* Hello, Mrs. Carver. Mother sent me on an errand.

AUNT SUE: Well, I'm glad she did. *(Leads* MARTHA *downstage)* I don't get to see my neighbors in Diamond Grove half often enough. *(*GEORGE *sets basket down outside door and comes in again, closing door behind him.)*

MARTHA *(Holding out package):* Mother made you a loaf of fresh corn bread.

AUNT SUE: How nice of her! She makes the best corn

bread I've ever tasted. *(She takes package and slips off string, which drops to floor as she pulls back paper.)* It looks delicious! *(She sets bread on table.* GEORGE *spies string and darts behind* AUNT SUE *to pick it up.)*

GEORGE: Aunt Sue, you dropped the string. *(He quickly winds string into little ball.)*

AUNT SUE: So I did. *(To* MARTHA*)* George is such a thrifty one! Saves everything. By the way, Martha, do you know our boy, George? George, this is Martha from the farm over the hill.

GEORGE: Afternoon, Martha.

MARTHA: Good afternoon, George. You're the one I've really come to see. Mother thought maybe you could do something about our garden. Everyone in town says you have such a way with plants.

AUNT SUE: That he has. I believe he was born with a green thumb. All green things seem to grow under his touch.

MARTHA *(Smiling; to* GEORGE*)*: I wish you could help us with our roses. We put them in last spring, and they did nicely for a while, but now the leaves are turning brown.

GEORGE: Maybe they don't get enough water or sunshine. I could tell if I saw them. *(Eagerly)* Could I go see them now, Aunt Sue?

AUNT SUE: Of course you may go, George, but not now. Your Uncle Mose will be wanting you to help him outside. Perhaps tomorrow. *(Door opens and* UNCLE MOSE, *a stern-looking white man, enters.)*

UNCLE MOSE *(Sharply):* George, where you have been?

AUNT SUE: Mose, we have a caller.

MARTHA: Afternoon, Mr. Carver.

UNCLE MOSE *(Turning):* Oh, how do you do, Martha?

(Turning back to GEORGE*)* George, didn't I tell you to finish chopping the wood this morning?

GEORGE *(Beginning to stammer):* I—I—I—

UNCLE MOSE *(Impatiently):* Well, answer me!

AUNT SUE *(More gently):* Did he tell you to do that, George?

GEORGE: Yes, Aunt Sue, but I—I forgot.

UNCLE MOSE: *Forgot?* Is that any excuse?

GEORGE: Oh, Aunt Sue, can't you make Uncle Mose understand? When I'm in the woods, I cannot think of anything but the plants, and the time passes so quickly. I didn't know it was so late.

AUNT SUE: He can do the work now, Mose. Go on, George. You'd better hurry.

GEORGE: Yes, Aunt Sue. *(He starts out.)*

UNCLE MOSE: The ax is by the door, and see that you use it this time.

GEORGE: Yes, Uncle Mose. *(He exits.)*

UNCLE MOSE *(To* MARTHA*)*: Susan makes excuses for the boy, and he *is* a good boy in many ways—but he must learn to do his work.

AUNT SUE: He's a big help with the cooking and cleaning, and when I put up preserves—

UNCLE MOSE: But what kind of work is that for a man? He has to learn to plow, so he'll be able to make a living. *(Sighs heavily)* Well, back to work. *(He turns to leave, then stops, turning to* MARTHA.*)* It was good to see you, Martha.

MARTHA: Good to see you, too, Mr. Carver. (UNCLE MOSE *exits and closes door.*)

AUNT SUE: Sit down, Martha.

MARTHA: Thank you. (MARTHA *sits on stool at left of table.* AUNT SUE *sits on stool at right.*)

AUNT SUE: You know, my husband does not mean to be
hard on the boy, but he does not always understand
George. He's been as good to George as if he were our
own son.

MARTHA: Has George always lived with you, Mrs. Carver?

AUNT SUE: Yes. Perhaps you're too young to remember
when we had all the trouble in Missouri between those
who believed in slavery and those who didn't.

MARTHA: I remember some of it, and I've heard stories.

AUNT SUE: Well, we were always against slavery. My
husband brought George's mother here—her name
was Mary. *(Sadly, remembering)* She was a fine girl.

MARTHA *(Tentatively):* Did she die?

AUNT SUE: We don't know. *(Sadly)* She was stolen by
night raiders, and we never saw her again.

MARTHA: How about George's father?

AUNT SUE: He was a slave on the Grant place—the
Baynhams own it now. Mose always wanted big
George to come here, too, so Mary and he could be
together, but we couldn't afford it. A few months before the raiders took Mary, big George was killed
while he was hauling wood.

MARTHA: And you kept the baby.

AUNT SUE: Yes, and his older brother, Jim. But Jim's
different. He's always been strong. He can do heavy
work, and he helps on other farms, too. George has
always been a bit sickly. His voice is still weak, and he
stammers sometimes.

MARTHA: But he's such a bright boy!

AUNT SUE *(Nodding):* It is remarkable. Why, it seems
he can do anything! *(She rises, goes to mantel and
picks up a long strip of knitting in different colors;*

showing it to MARTHA) Look at this. George is knitting it.

MARTHA *(Surprised)*: Knitting? *(Examining it)* It's beautiful work.

AUNT SUE: Yes—and I never taught him. He was watching me one day and said, "Aunt Sue, I could do that." Later, he made some needles from turkey feathers and sat down and started this. *(Puts knitting back on mantel)*

MARTHA: He seems to be able to do anything with his hands! How do you account for his knowing so much about plants?

AUNT SUE: No one can account for that. It's just—well, uncanny. And it seems he's always searching to learn more. *(Door opens suddenly, and* GEORGE *runs in, followed by* UNCLE MOSE. GEORGE *carries a branch and is obviously frightened.* UNCLE MOSE *is angry and catches hold of* GEORGE's *shoulder, but* GEORGE *breaks away and runs to* AUNT SUE.)

UNCLE MOSE *(Angrily)*: Don't you go whimpering to your aunt. She won't save you this time! *(He grabs* GEORGE *by the arm and pulls him away from* AUNT SUE.)

AUNT SUE: Mose, you're hurting the boy! (MARTHA *looks frightened.*)

UNCLE MOSE: Susan, the boy is to be punished this time—and severely!

GEORGE *(Stammering)*: P—p—please, Aunt Sue.

AUNT SUE: What has he done, Mose?

UNCLE MOSE: Instead of chopping the wood as I told him, he took the ax and started chopping at our finest apple tree!

AUNT SUE *(Shocked)*: But George wouldn't hurt a tree!

UNCLE MOSE (*Pointing at branch* GEORGE *is holding*): There's your proof—right in his hand. The apple branch he chopped off!

AUNT SUE (*Shocked*): George! There must have been some reason—

UNCLE MOSE (*Loudly*): Reason? You talk of reason?

GEORGE (*Stammering*): Aunt Sue, I—I—tried—to—to—tell him. (*Holds up branch*) S—see?

AUNT SUE: Tell him what, George?

GEORGE: I—I wanted to—to show him, but he—he wouldn't listen.

AUNT SUE: George, wait a minute, child. You're so excited, I can't understand you.

UNCLE MOSE: Susan, you're always making excuses for the boy.

AUNT SUE: Mose, you know George stammers when he's overexcited. He loses his voice. (*Calmly; to* GEORGE) George, try to tell me.

GEORGE (*Holding out branch*): B-bugs, Aunt Sue, b—bugs all over the branch!

AUNT SUE (*Peering at branch*): What? What's that?

GEORGE (*More calmly, speaking more plainly*): Tiny bugs crawling on it, see?

AUNT SUE: So there are. Look, Mose, little bugs. You can hardly see them.

UNCLE MOSE (*Examining branch*): Why, you're right.

GEORGE: I—I tried to tell you, Uncle Mose. (*To* AUNT SUE) I ran to him, Aunt Sue, and I pulled at him, but he wouldn't listen. He kept telling me to chop the wood.

UNCLE MOSE: I couldn't understand him, Susan.

GEORGE: The bugs would spread and kill the tree. I—I had to do something.

MARTHA *(Moving toward* GEORGE *and looking at branch):* Why, I believe these are the same bugs that attacked one of our trees at home, and the tree died!

UNCLE MOSE *(Embarrassed):* I don't know what to say. I've looked at that tree a dozen times, and I didn't see them.

MARTHA: But George did!

AUNT SUE: Oh, Mose, it's just as I've tried to tell you. The boy has some great gift. Small as he is, he sees things we don't see—about plants, about many things.

UNCLE MOSE: I'm beginning to believe you're right, Susan.

AUNT SUE *(Firmly):* And he must go to school so that he can learn.

MARTHA *(To* UNCLE MOSE): There's a school in Neosho, the county seat, where they would take him.

GEORGE *(Eagerly):* Oh, Aunt Sue—Uncle Mose . . . I'd do anything if I could go to school!

UNCLE MOSE: It will be hard for the boy—alone. Neosho is so far away. He couldn't come back here at night to eat and sleep.

GEORGE: I don't care if I have to sleep in a barn or outside or anywhere, Uncle Mose, if only I can go to school.

AUNT SUE: I think you can earn your way, George. You could do odd jobs. (GEORGE *nods enthusiastically.*)

UNCLE MOSE *(Worriedly):* But he is so young, and too small to be on his own.

AUNT SUE *(Firmly):* It is what he must do. *(She puts her hand on* GEORGE's *arm.)* I have a strong feeling that he will keep on learning more and more—that he will do wonderful things—that he will be a great man. *(Curtain)*

* * * * *

SCENE 2

TIME: *The summer of 1896.*

SETTING: *Classroom at Iowa State College. At center is large desk facing left. Books, papers, file boxes for slides, and a microscope are on desk. At right of desk is a swivel chair; at left of desk are two students' desks and chairs. Above desk hang some botanical charts.*

AT RISE: GEORGE WASHINGTON CARVER, *now in his early thirties, is studying a chart. He has a moustache twisted at the ends. His plain suit of clothes is well worn, and in the buttonhole of his coat he wears a flower. After a moment, he turns and starts toward desk, sees something on floor, and stoops to pick it up. It is a piece of string. He opens desk drawer, takes out a ball of string and winds piece on it, then puts ball back in drawer. He sits down at desk and studies a slide through microscope. He takes slide out, puts it in box and makes a notation on a piece of paper. There is a knock on door.*

CARVER: Come in. *(He puts another slide under microscope, and* JAMES G. WILSON, *a middle-aged white professor, enters.)*

WILSON: Well, George, I see you're working late, as usual.

CARVER *(Starting to rise):* Oh, Professor Wilson.

WILSON: Don't get up. (CARVER *sits down again.*) You ought to be celebrating tonight, now that you are to receive your master's degree. George Washington Carver—Bachelor of Science, Master of Science.

CARVER: I *am* celebrating, working on my mycological collection. It's never been properly catalogued before.

WILSON *(Picking up a slide and looking at it):* A great collection. How many specimens are there now?

CARVER: Over twenty thousand.

WILSON: George, that's wonderful! (WILSON *pulls up chair and sits opposite* GEORGE.) You've traveled a long, hard road, George.

CARVER: It has been long, sir, but I don't know about hard.

WILSON *(Shaking his head):* I don't know how you did it. Going to school in so many different places, traveling from town to town, working at odd jobs—with no family of your own.

CARVER: But in a way I did have families, sir, many families. People were always so kind. The Carvers treated me as their own son, and in Neosho Aunt Mariah Watkins took me in. Then there were the Seymours and the Milhollands, and last but not least, all of you here at Ames.

WILSON *(Smiling):* Ames was fortunate indeed that you came here. Iowa State College has never had a more brilliant student, and your work here these last two years on the faculty as an assistant botanist has been outstanding.

CARVER: I couldn't have done it without your help.

WILSON: It seems to me you've always helped yourself most of all. The way you've worked—waiting on tables, doing laundry, anything you could put your hands to.

CARVER: But I enjoy working with my hands.

WILSON: And a good thing, since you have to earn your own way.

CARVER: But think of all you've done for me, Professor Wilson—buying the ticket for me to go to that art exhibit, seeing that my paintings got hung—

WILSON: Well, that was certainly worthwhile. Weren't

your paintings chosen to hang in the World's Colum-
bian Exposition?

CARVER *(Musing):* Ah, my paintings. You know, ever
since I was a boy I've thought perhaps I'd like to be a
great artist and go to Paris to study. There's always
been a conflict between that and my work with plants,
but there isn't time for everything.

WILSON: Have you given up the idea of studying art?

CARVER: Yes, sir. I feel I can be of more service to others
in agriculture.

WILSON: That's like you, George, to think of what you
can do for others. You have so many talents, but
there's no one who can touch you in the field of agriculture. Your work with grafting, cross-breeding and
hybridization has been recognized by authorities all
over the country. And now the final step, George.
(After a pause) You're to be given a full professorship
here at Ames.

CARVER *(Overwhelmed):* It's a honor, sir, but I'm afraid
I can't accept.

WILSON *(Astonished):* Why not?

CARVER: You knew that Booker T. Washington of
Tuskegee Institute in Alabama had written, asking me
to be in charge of their agriculture department.

WILSON: Yes, but I didn't know you were considering it
seriously.

CARVER: I feel I must go.

WILSON: But Tuskegee offered you only fifteen hundred
dollars a year. That's not a large salary, George.

CARVER: No, but money is not important to me. My
needs are few.

WILSON *(Laughing a little):* True. No one could ever
accuse you of wasting your money. But George, have

you thought over what it will mean to you? Here we have all the most modern equipment—you can go on with your experiments.

CARVER: I expect to continue with my experiments at Tuskegee.

WILSON: But they have so little laboratory equipment!

CARVER: I know that, and Mr. Washington realizes it, too.

WILSON: Then how can you do as much there?

CARVER (*Fervently*): There must be a way! Alabama has soil, sunshine, and rain—it will be a challenge for me. I'm certain that land can produce a living for all its people!

WILSON (*Shaking his head*): Well, if there is anything in that land, you're the man to find it! (*Upset*) But I just can't think of your leaving Ames. I always thought your future should be here.

CARVER: Perhaps if you read Mr. Washington's letter, you'd understand, Professor Wilson. (*He takes a letter from his coat pocket and hands it to* WILSON.)

WILSON (*Scanning the letter*): "Hm—m . . . (*Reads*) "The students, barefoot, come for miles over bad roads. They are thin and in rags. You would not understand such poverty." (WILSON *looks up at* CARVER *and smiles*.) Mr. Washington evidently doesn't know much about your background, George.

CARVER: No, I guess he doesn't.

WILSON (*Reading*): "I cannot offer you money, position or fame. I offer you in their place work—hard, hard work—the task of bringing a people from degradation, poverty, and waste to full manhood." (WILSON *looks at* CARVER *in silence for a moment*.) George, you have made the only decision that you could make. This is something bigger than personal ambition.

CARVER *(Smiling):* I'm glad you understand.

WILSON: All of us who know you best will understand. We here at Ames will miss you and your work, but we must recognize what you must do.

CARVER: Thank you, Professor Wilson. It will make it easier for me knowing my friends approve the step I'm taking. (WILSON *shakes his hand.*)

WILSON: Our blessings go with you, and I know all your efforts will be crowned with success. *(Curtain)*

* * * * *

SCENE 3

TIME: *1937.*

SETTING: *Carver's study at Tuskegee. Large window with many plants in window box is center. Books line walls on either side of window. On side walls hang many pictures and embroideries. Door is down. left; upstage from door is glass case containing geological collection. Large, old desk, piled high with papers and books, is against right wall; there is a microscope on desk and a push button on side of desk. In front of desk is a chair; next to desk is a wastebasket. Large table piled with miscellaneous collection of geological specimens and magnifying glass is center. There are chairs about the room, and every corner is crammed with plants, pieces of embroidery, specimens, etc.*

AT RISE: CARVER *is working on plant. His hair and moustache are white, and his shoulders are bent. His clothes look well-worn; he wears a flower in the buttonhole of his lapel. He lifts plant from table and examines it; picking up magnifying glass, he exam-*

ines plant more closely. The door opens left and black SECRETARY *enters. She carries sheet of paper in one hand and bundle of mail tied with a piece of string in the other.*

SECRETARY: Good morning, Dr. Carver.

CARVER: Good morning.

SECRETARY: Here's the mail—over a hundred letters again today.

CARVER: My, my, think of that. It always surprises me how many people find time to write. *(Chuckling)* They always start by saying how busy they know I am and then they go on for pages.

SECRETARY: And it's such work for you, Doctor, to go through them all. I could take care of some of it for you.

CARVER: Yes, I daresay you could, but the truth is I like reading them. Besides, I've been answering letters like this for so many years that when they ask questions about their soil or water or crops, I know just what they mean.

SECRETARY: Yes, I suppose you are the only one who can do it, but there are so many other things—*(She consults the sheet of paper.)* You've a very busy day ahead.

CARVER: Is that so? *(He takes another plant from table and looks at it admiringly.)* You know, I had a very successful walk this morning—seventeen different varieties—now, look at this, did you ever see a more beautiful specimen?

SECRETARY *(Smiling):* It's a fine specimen, Doctor, but your list of appointments—*(She holds out list.)*

CARVER: *(Putting down plant):* Oh, very well. What do we have today? *(He walks over to desk and sits down facing her, folding his hands in a resigned manner.)*

SECRETARY *(Consulting sheet):* Well, at eleven o'clock,

you're to meet with that committee from Washington—something about dehydration.

CARVER: Ah, yes, I've been preaching dehydration for thirty years, and now the bigwigs are really interested. You'd think it was the first time they had ever heard of it.

SECRETARY: And then that Horticultural Society is visiting here today. You promised to speak to them at one o'clock.

CARVER: So I did.

SECRETARY *(Consulting list again):* There's a man from California who wants to know something about the paints you've made from our Alabama clay.

CARVER: Oh, yes, he owns a large paint company, and he's going to offer me a lot of money to go to work for him.

SECRETARY *(Anxiously):* Doctor, we're not going to lose you, are we?

CARVER *(Smiling):* No, you're not. I'm not in the business of making money. I wouldn't know what to do with it if I made it by the bushel. Well, is that all?

SECRETARY: No—right now there are two reporters waiting to interview you. That's the first thing.

CARVER *(Shaking his head):* Oh, my, I don't like talking to reporters.

SECRETARY: I know, but they say their paper's been trying to get a story for a long time about the—*(She stops and smiles.)* the Wizard of Tuskegee.

CARVER *(Smiling, too, but shaking his head):* Wizard of Tuskegee? Well, I'll set them right on that. Show them in.

SECRETARY: Yes, Doctor. *(She unties bundle of letters, drops string in wastebasket, and puts bundle on desk.)* Here's your mail. *(She turns and exits.* CARVER *reaches into wastebasket and pulls out string. He opens desk drawer, takes out ball of string, and carefully winds piece around. He puts ball back into drawer as* SECRETARY *enters, followed by two white* REPORTERS, *who carry notebooks and pencils.)*

SECRETARY: Dr. Carver, these are the gentlemen from the *Courier.*

REPORTERS: Good morning, Doctor.

CARVER: Good morning, gentlemen. Won't you sit down? *(He motions to chairs near table.* REPORTERS *sit.* SECRETARY *exits left.)*

CARVER: Well, now that you've cornered me in my lair, what can I do for you?

1ST REPORTER: Well, sir, there have been so many things printed about what you've done that we thought we'd like to get the story of your life.

CARVER *(Humorously):* Dear me, that's a large order. There are so many ramifications. Perhaps if you would just ask me questions . . .

2ND REPORTER: Of course, we know about all the honors you've received—the degrees, the Springarn Medal—

1ST REPORTER: And all the fine offers you've had. Didn't Edison want you to work for him once? *(During following dialogue,* REPORTERS *periodically take notes.)*

CARVER: Yes, he did.

1ST REPORTER: Would you care to quote the salary he offered?

CARVER *(Hesitating):* No. No, I wouldn't, but if it's of great interest to you, it was six figures.

1ST REPORTER *(Impressed):* A hundred thousand dollars is a lot of money, sir. What made you turn it down?

CARVER: Well, you see, I have no real use for that kind of money. I wanted to stay on here at Tuskegee—besides, I'd promised Booker T. Washington that I would.

2ND REPORTER: You were very close to Mr. Washington, weren't you?

CARVER: Yes, we worked together for many years. We watched Tuskegee grow from a poor, struggling school to the fine institution it is today.

1ST REPORTER: Are you still teaching, Dr. Carver?

CARVER: No. Mr. Washington released me from my teaching duties before he died, so that I could spend all my time on research. But I still keep my eye on the students. You see, I'm still a student myself. Every day I learn something—why, you take these specimens I picked up this morning—*(He rises and goes to table, stopping abruptly)* Oh, dear—

2ND REPORTER: Is something wrong, sir?

CARVER: No—but you'll have to excuse me for a moment. I've forgotten something. *(He picks up a plant, goes to desk, taking specimen with him. He scribbles something on a scrap of paper.)* You see, I discovered a very rare species of fungi this morning—I must send it to the United States Department of Agriculture right away. *(He presses button at side of desk.)*

2ND REPORTER: A new species? *(With pencil poised)* What is it?

CARVER *(Dryly; rattling it off):* Why, it's a specimen of Pandanus javanicus variegatus attacked by Diplodia natalansis.

2ND REPORTER: Oh, I see. (SECRETARY *enters.*)

SECRETARY: Yes, Dr. Carver?

CARVER: Will you take this to the laboratory? Ask Mr. Curtis to have it prepared and sent off at once. *(He hands her note and specimen.)*

SECRETARY: Yes, sir. *(She exits left.)*

CARVER: Please excuse the interruption, gentlemen. I noticed you eyeing my cluttered desk. *(Gestures)* It's rather dreadful—I once had an assistant who classified this conglomeration as orderly disorder.

2ND REPORTER *(Laughing):* Well, it does look a little confusing.

CARVER: But I really can find things, you know. *(He delves into pile of papers and comes up triumphantly with a few small envelopes.)* Here, for instance, are some packets of flower seeds that have to go off today.

2ND REPORTER: Are you sending them to some horticultural society?

CARVER: No, just to friends. *(As he holds up packet)* These go to a lady six miles from here, and these to a gentleman in Arizona, and these to a professor in Germany.

1ST REPORTER *(Pointing to paintings on wall):* These paintings are your own work, aren't they, Dr. Carver? I've heard you're an artist. *(Rises to examine them more closely)*

CARVER: Yes, but I haven't had much time to spend on my painting since coming to Tuskegee. I did most of these to show the students what could be done with the colors in Alabama clay.

1ST REPORTER: Pigments from clay? *(Stopping before a still life)* This is a fine study.

CARVER: Ah, yes. That illustrates a new techinique. I did it with my fingertips instead of a brush.

1ST REPORTER *(Impressed):* Amazing. *(Pointing to one of the embroideries on wall)* I see you have some beautiful samples of embroidery—are they of some particular interest?

CARVER: Oh, not really. I make them from time to time for relaxation.

1ST REPORTER *(Surprised): You* make them?

CARVER: Yes, I learned to do it when I was a boy. (2ND REPORTER *rises, looks into case up left.)*

2ND REPORTER: What's in the case, Dr. Carver? It looks like a diamond!

CARVER *(Crossing to join* 2ND REPORTER): It is. There are many varieties of native quartz, and one of them happens to be a diamond.

1ST REPORTER *(As he looks at diamond):* Isn't that worth a lot of money?

CARVER: Oh, I expect it is. How I came by it is rather amusing. You see, I'd helped a gentleman who manufactures peanut butter. He'd had trouble with the oil rising to the top, and I showed him how to avoid that. He was so grateful he asked me what I wanted. I told him I'd like a diamond, so he sent it to me, mounted in a beautiful ring.

2ND REPORTER *(Amused):* He thought you wanted to wear it.

CARVER: Of course, and I guess he was a little taken aback when he found I'd put it in my geological collection.

1ST REPORTER *(Laughing):* No wonder. *(All sit.)*

2ND REPORTER: Peanuts are one of your specialties, aren't they, Doctor?

CARVER: Gentlemen, you can make most anything from the peanut. When I first started working on peanuts, I was amazed.

2ND REPORTER: How many products have you developed?

CARVER: Over three hundred, including milk, cream,

coffee, paper, stains, plastics—

1ST REPORTER: Plastics? That's becoming an important industry now, isn't it?

CARVER: Yes, it is, but twenty years ago we were making what they call plastics today from peanuts, sweet potatoes, and many other plants right here at Tuskegee.

2ND REPORTER: I didn't realize that.

CARVER: I find that with most scientific developments there is a lapse of about twenty years between the laboratory work and actually putting the knowledge to use. (SECRETARY *enters left.*)

SECRETARY: Excuse me, Dr. Carver—

CARVER: Yes?

SECRETARY: I don't like to bother you, but there's a young man here who insists on seeing you. He says it will only take a minute.

CARVER: Very well. I'm sure these gentlemen won't mind.

1ST REPORTER: Of course not. (SECRETARY *starts for door, then turns back.*)

SECRETARY: Oh, and there's another thing. The treasurer's office called about your salary checks that are still uncashed. The auditors are coming soon, and they'd like you to cash your checks so they can balance the books.

CARVER: Dear me, we had the same trouble last year, didn't we?

SECRETARY *(Shaking her head, gently reprimanding him):* Yes, we did, Dr. Carver.

CARVER: I know they're all here somewhere. In fact, I saw one just this morning. *(He dives into pile of papers on desk and brings up a check.)* You see? A nice, fresh one—it's only six months old!

SECRETARY *(Shaking her head; smiling):* I'll send the young man in. *(She exits.)*

CARVER: I suppose I should try to be more careful, but there's not much sense cashing these checks unless I need the money, and I can't spend fifteen hundred dollars a year.

2ND REPORTER *(Surprised):* Fifteen hundred! You mean that's your salary here?

CARVER: Why, yes. It's the amount Mr. Washington offered me when I came here in 1896, and I've been getting it ever since.

1ST REPORTER: It's not very much.

CARVER *(Laughing):* Well, I guess if they thought I was worth more they'd pay me more. *(He pauses; then laughing)* I'm only making a joke, gentlemen. They've tried to increase my salary, but, well, you see, I don't need what I have. It seems to me people place an exaggerated importance on money. *(He stops, seeing* YOUNG MAN, *black, standing in doorway.)* Oh, come in. I'm delighted to see you. (CARVER *crosses to greet* YOUNG MAN, *shakes his hand. Then with one hand on his shoulder, he draws* YOUNG MAN *down center.)*

YOUNG MAN: Thank you, Professor Carver. I'm sorry to interrupt like this, but I didn't have much time.

CARVER: Not much time? Well, that's good. That shows you're busy.

YOUNG MAN: Yes sir, I am, but the last time I saw you, you told me to come back and report—about the dollar you gave me.

CARVER: So I did. Well, what have you done with it?

YOUNG MAN: Well, I bought a hen for fifty cents and a setting of eggs for fifteen—the rest I used for feed.

CARVER *(Nodding his head):* Yes . . .

YOUNG MAN: Well, the eggs hatched out all right, and

then *(Excitedly)* some more and then some more—well, now, sir, I've got seventy-five hens bringing in money. You wouldn't believe it, Professor Carver, but now I've saved up fifty-one dollars, and I'm going to pay it down on a lot.

CARVER: Fine. You've got a start on a place of your own. That's what I like to see.

YOUNG MAN: I have to go now. There's a bus leaving in a few minutes.

CARVER: Let me know when you have two hundred chickens! Goodbye. (YOUNG MAN *exits.* CARVER *turns back to* REPORTERS.)

1ST REPORTER: That young man seems to be doing all right.

CARVER: Of course he is! Now, that's what I call a proper expenditure of money. By adding a little common sense and a lot of hard work to that dollar, he's made something worthwhile out of it.

2ND REPORTER: He certainly didn't waste any of it.

CARVER: No waste. That's the secret. There need never be waste. It's what we have been teaching here ever since this school began. And by doing just that, we have prospered.

1ST REPORTER: It's wonderful.

CARVER: Everything has a purpose—even a weed.

2ND REPORTER: Then why don't we make use of the weeds?

CARVER: We will. In fact, we have, here at Tuskegee. A weed is simply a plant growing where we don't want it to grow. If we cultivate it properly, it can be used. And it's the same with all other forms of waste. Corn stalks, peanut shells, wood shavings—

1ST REPORTER: You've made marble from wood shavings, haven't you, Doctor?

CARVER: Yes, and that's only one thing. Some day all the

waste products of agriculture will be used in industry. There is untold wealth lying all about us, if we will but look for it—a fourth kingdom, I like to call it. (SECRE-TARY *enters left.)*

SECRETARY: Dr. Carver, I'm sorry for all these interruptions, but there are two little boys outside with a very sick dog.

CARVER: A dog?

SECRETARY: Yes. They have walked miles lugging the poor animal, and they say if the "Professor" will just look at him, he'll be all right.

CARVER *(Laughing):* I'm sorry, gentlemen. You'll have to excuse me again. *(They smile as he crosses left and follows* SECRETARY *out.)*

1ST REPORTER *(Shaking his head):* What a man!

2ND REPORTER: He's amazing—doing the finest creative research in the country, and he takes time to look at a sick dog!

1ST REPORTER *(Rising and walking about; enthusiastically):* Well, we've got a story. Do you see it the way I do? It's not so much the honors he's received or the big things he's done—it's just one human being working for the good of all the others.

2ND REPORTER: That's it exactly. Why, the whole story of his life is one of service to others. He lives it every day.

1ST REPORTER: And that's what we want to write about. He hasn't given us any dates, but we can easily look them up in *Who's Who.*

2ND REPORTER *(Rising):* Sure, there's a copy right on the shelves here. I wonder what it says about him. *(He takes copy of* Who's Who in America *from shelf and thumbs through it.)* Here it is! *(Reads)* "Carver, George Washington—born a slave, 1864—worked way through high school, Minneapolis, Kansas, and later through college—B.S. Agriculture, Iowa State College, 1894—M.S. Agriculture, 1896. Member of Royal Society of Arts, London—"*(He stops, looks up.)* Born a slave—made a member of the Royal Society of Arts in London. I'll bet he's the only one who ever bridged that gap! *(He shuts book and puts it back on shelf. CARVER re-enters, smiling.)*

1ST REPORTER: Well, Doctor? How's the dog?

CARVER: A slight case of distemper, but he'll live. In fact, we're going to keep him right here for a few days, until he recovers.

1ST REPORTER: Dr. Carver, I think we've taken up enough of your time.

CARVER: Well, I—I haven't told you very much, I'm afraid.

2ND REPORTER: Oh, we have our story all right. Thanks so much, Doctor, for giving us the interview.

CARVER: You're entirely welcome. *(They shake hands; REPORTERS start to exit left.)*

1ST REPORTER *(Turning):* Oh, by the way, Dr. Carver, is there any particular statement you'd like to make?

CARVER *(Smiling):* There is one thing, gentlemen. Please don't refer to me as a wizard. I'm not one, you know.

1ST REPORTER: Very well, sir. We won't. We'll just tell the truth. We'll say that you're a truly great man. *(They exit. CARVER walks toward stage center, shaking his head.)*

CARVER: Great man—humph! Now, let me see—where was I? Oh, yes. *(He walks to table, takes a plant from basket, picks up magnifying glass, examines plant as curtain falls.)*

THE END

PRODUCTION NOTES

GEORGE WASHINGTON CARVER

Characters: 7 male; 3 female.

Playing Time: 40 minutes.

Costumes: All characters wear clothes appropriate to periods represented. Carver's clothes are a bit shabby, and he always wears flower in buttonhole.

Properties: Scene 1: Basket filled with plants, grasses, flat stone; package tied with string containing loaf of bread; branch. Scene 3: Sheet of paper; bundle of mail tied with string; notebooks and pencils.

Setting: Scene 1: Interior of log house. There is a door up center and a window in left wall. At right is a rough fireplace with cooking utensils hanging near it and a rough mantel above it. There are pieces of pewter and a roll of knitting on mantel. There are two wooden beds against upstage wall on either side of door and a table at center. Around table are two or three stools. A spinning wheel and stool stand downstage. Scene 2: Classroom at Iowa State College. At center is a large desk facing left. Books, papers, file boxes for slides, and a microscope are on desk. At right of desk is swivel chair; at left of desk are two students' desks and chairs. Above desk hang botanical charts. There is a piece of string on floor and a ball of string in desk drawer. Scene 3: Carver's study at Tuskegee. Large window with many plants in window box is center. Books line walls on either side of window. On side walls hang many pictures and embroideries. Door is downstage left; upstage from door is glass case containing geological collection. Large, old desk, piled high with papers and books, is against right wall; there is a microscope on desk and a push button on side of desk. In front of desk is a chair and down from desk is a wastebasket. Large table piled with miscellaneous collection of geological specimens and magnifying glass is center. There are chairs about the room, and every corner is crammed with plants, pieces of embroidery, specimens, etc.

Lighting and Sound: No special effects.

John Henry

by Barbara Winther

Characters

BALLAD SINGER
POLLY ANNE
LITTLE BILL
JOHN HENRY
SAM, *the salesman*
CAPTAIN TOMMY
TWO MEN
TWO WOMEN
PEOPLE, *extras*

AUTHOR'S NOTE

The Swannanoa tunnel, built in West Virginia in the 1880's, was the longest and most difficult tunnel ever cut through a mountain. It was on this tunnel that John Henry, a legendary black man, was supposed to have worked. John became the hero of the southern working men, especially railroad builders, who sang about his strength and his courage as they worked. The ballad, with its many verses telling the exploits of John Henry, is the basis for this play.

SCENE 1

BEFORE RISE: BALLAD SINGER, *carrying guitar, enters in front of curtain, playing and singing to tune of folk song "John Henry," with interjections from* PEOPLE *offstage.*

SINGER: John Henry was a black man hero,

PEOPLE: Uh-huh!

SINGER: Born in West Virginia, they say.

PEOPLE: That's right!

SINGER: He could split a boulder with a hammer,

PEOPLE: Hallelujah!

SINGER: And he grew to a man in one day.

PEOPLE: Praise the Lord.

SINGER: And he grew to a man in one day. *(Speaking, as* PEOPLE *hum in background)* Then John Henry took his twenty-pound hammer, said goodbye to his mammy and pappy and started off across the United States. He was hunting for something. He didn't know what—happiness, maybe, or peace in his soul. All over the country he worked, using his hammer to lay tracks for the railroads. *(Sound of train whistle is heard, followed by rhythmic sound of steel hitting steel, continuing until curtain opens.* SINGER *resumes singing, as before, and* PEOPLE *sing from offstage.)* John Henry had a little woman.

PEOPLE: Uh-huh!

SINGER: Polly Anne was her name.

PEOPLE: That's right!

SINGER: And he worked on the Big Bend Tunnel.

PEOPLE: Oh, yeah!

SINGER: Where his courage and strength brought him fame.

PEOPLE: Hallelujah. (SINGER *starts to exit.*)

SINGER: Where his courage and strength brought him fame. *(Exits. Curtain opens.)*

*   *   *   *   *

TIME: *Late afternoon, 1880.*

SETTING: *A country hillside in the southern United States. There is a backdrop painting of hills and forest, with a winding railroad track going through a tunnel, which gives the appearance of leading off right. At center are two tree stumps used as seats.*

AT RISE: POLLY ANNE *enters left and crosses right where she looks off, squinting.* LITTLE BILL *wearily enters right, carrying jacket over shoulder. He tips his cap as he approaches her.*

BILL: Afternoon, Polly Anne.

POLLY: Afternoon, Little Bill. Is John Henry on his way home?

BILL: Your husband is coming up the hill. *(Sits on stump and wipes forehead with bandana)* Whew! I'm worn out. Glad this work day is over.

POLLY *(Wagging her finger, playfully):* Little Bill, all you do is hold the drills while John pounds them into the ground. He does the work while you just watch.

BILL: But John works twice as hard as anyone else, so I have to hold twice as many drills and watch twice as much happen. *(She laughs.* JOHN *enters, carrying hammer.)*

JOHN: Hi, Polly Anne. What's for supper?

POLLY: Three kettles of black-eyed peas, two roast pigs, five possums, a mountain of sweet potatoes, a couple of hills of turnip greens, two hundred biscuits, and five kegs of honey.

JOHN: Sounds mighty good, but I'm powerfully hungry. I doubt that'll be enough to carry me until breakfast.

POLLY *(Shaking head; good-naturedly):* John Henry, your stomach is a bottomless pit. Dinner time is in five minutes—and you'd better bring a shovel. *(Grins and exits)*

JOHN: You know, Little Bill *(Placing foot on other stump and resting elbow on knee),* for the first time in my life I am a contented man. I like living here and working on the railroad for Captain Tommy.

BILL: Captain's a fair man, as bosses go.

JOHN *(Nodding):* That's the truth. *(Crossing right)* See you in the morning, Bill.

BILL: Sure enough, John. (JOHN *exits.* BILL *rises, rubbing shoulder muscles.* SAM *enters left.)*

SAM: Hey, there—you.

BILL: What is it, stranger?

SAM: I'm looking for a man called Captain Tommy.

BILL: You'll find him at the bottom of the hill. *(Points right)*

SAM: Good. *(Hooking thumbs in suspenders, swaggering)* I suspect you'll be seeing a lot of me around here. I've invented something that will change the lives of everyone who works on the railroad.

BILL: What's that?

SAM: Wouldn't do to tell my secret to you. *(Salutes cockily)* Wait until tomorrow. *(Exits right)*

BILL: I don't like the looks of that fellow. I have a feeling something bad is about to happen. *(Train whistle blows as curtain closes.)*

* * * * *

SCENE 2

BEFORE RISE: CAPTAIN TOMMY, *holding paper, with pencil behind ear, enters in front of curtain and stands center, reading silently as lights go up.* SAM *enters left.*

SAM: Are you Captain Tommy?

CAPTAIN: I am.

SAM: Permit me to introduce myself. I am Sam, superior salesman and owner of Johnson's Steam Drill Company.

CAPTAIN: I'm not buying any newfangled gadgets. *(Starts to write on paper)*

SAM: Wait a bit, Captain. Suppose I tell you I've invented a machine that can drive more holes than twenty men, without resting.

CAPTAIN *(Not looking up):* I'd say you were crazier than a bedbug and ought to soak your head in a bucket of water.

SAM *(Crossing arms):* I have this machine here, sir, and I am willing to show you how fantastic it is.

CAPTAIN *(Slowly looking up):* Well, I suppose I could take a look at your invention. *(Narrowing eyes)* How do I know it can do what you claim?

SAM: By testing it. *(Coming closer)* Who is your strongest working man?

CAPTAIN: John Henry, without a doubt. *(Tucks pencil behind ear)*

SAM: I've heard of him.

CAPTAIN: The finest steel-driving man in the country.

SAM: Captain, I propose a race between my steam drill and your worker, John Henry.

CAPTAIN: How long a race?

SAM: Nine hours.

CAPTAIN: What? You can't expect a man to drive steel for nine hours.

SAM: Of course not. I expect to show you that my machine will still be working long after John Henry quits.

CAPTAIN: Hm-m-m. I don't know. I'll have to ask John. *(Musing)* Of course, he's never turned his back on a challenge.

SAM *(Extending hand):* Agreed, then?

CAPTAIN: If John wants to do it, it's agreeable with me. *(Clasping SAM's hand)* If your steam drill wins, then I'll buy it. If your steam drill loses—

SAM: Yes?

CAPTAIN: Then you have to pay me five hundred dollars.

SAM *(Smiling):* Captain, you drive a hard bargain—but I can't possibly lose, so I accept your terms. *(They shake hands.)* My steam drill will be ready to go in the morning. *(Exits left. CAPTAIN starts to write.)*

CAPTAIN: City slickers think their machines have all the answers. *(Looking after SAM)* Who knows? Maybe they do. *(Blackout. CAPTAIN exits. Spotlight comes up on SINGER, who enters with guitar and plays and sings as before. PEOPLE sing from offstage.)*

SINGER: Well, the Captain said to John Henry,
Shall we bring that steam drill around?
Will you race nine hours out on the job,
Driving steel on into the ground?

PEOPLE: Hallelujah.

SINGER: Driving steel on into the ground?

PEOPLE: Then John Henry said to his captain,

SINGER: Well, a man ain't nothing but a man,
But before I let that steam drill beat me down,

PEOPLE: I'll die with a hammer in my hand.

SINGER: Praise the Lord!

PEOPLE: I'll die with a hammer in my hand. *(Spotlight goes out. SINGER exits. Curtain opens. Lights come up.)*

* * * * *

SCENE 3

TIME: *Late morning, the next day.*

SETTING: *Same as Scene 1.*

AT RISE: *Stage is empty.* JOHN, *carrying hammer,* BILL *and* POLLY *enter left.*

JOHN: Little Bill, will you hold the drills for me in the race?

BILL: I've been doing that for you ever since you came here, John. I won't desert you now.

POLLY: How can I help, John?

JOHN: By bringing me water. I imagine I'll be feeling pretty thirsty as I work.

POLLY: All right. *(Touching* JOHN's *shoulder)* Are you certain you want to enter this race? (JOHN *nods.)* Everyone knows you're the greatest steel-driving man that ever lived. You don't have to prove it. But, John, if a machine breaks down, it can be repaired so it can go on working forever. *(Gently)* But *you* can't go on working forever.

JOHN: No, but I can show how a man can strive for what he cares about. Working on this railroad has been the happiest time of my life. I'm not going to sit back and let a machine take that work away from me, or from others who feel the same way I do about the railroad.

BILL *(To* POLLY): We have to let him do it, Polly Anne. *(Exits right)*

POLLY: I know, Little Bill. I'm just frightened for him. Worried and frightened. *(Exits right, followed by* BILL. CAPTAIN *and* PEOPLE *enter left, humming to tune of "John Henry," as they take places to watch the race. Some point and peer off right, nodding and gesturing to each other. Others may lay blanket on ground, for a picnic.* TWO WOMEN *with open parasols and fancy dresses are escorted by* TWO MEN *to tree stumps, where they sit. By the time the song is hummed through once, all have found places on stage.)*

CAPTAIN *(Shouting off):* On your mark, get set *(Pause)*, go. *(Blast of train whistle and then sound of steel hitting steel and chugging of steam engine continue until race is over. Crowd cheers.)*

1ST MAN: Look at John Henry go with that hammer!

2ND MAN: But the steam drill's going just as fast.

1ST WOMAN: And this is a nine-hour race.

2ND WOMAN: John will wear himself out.

1ST WOMAN: I don't see how he can keep up this pace.

1ST MAN: You can bet he'll use every ounce of strength he's got.

2ND MAN: He can't beat a machine.

1ST MAN: Maybe not, but he's got the courage to try.

PEOPLE *(Cheering; ad lib):* Come on, John Henry. You can do it! *(Etc.)*

2ND WOMAN: We're rooting for you.

PEOPLE *(Chanting):* John Henry, John Henry, John Henry . . . *(Chanting fades as lights dim. Spotlight comes up on* SINGER *as he re-enters, playing and singing as before.)*

SINGER: Sunshine was hot and burning,
Wasn't a breeze at all,
Sweat ran down like water down a hill,
That day John Henry let his hammer fall,
Lord! Lord!
That day John Henry let his hammer fall.
(Spotlight goes out. SINGER *exits.* POLLY *enters and stands at right with* CAPTAIN, *so that they can speak to* JOHN, *who is just offstage right.* PEOPLE *begin chanting softly again, as lights go up gradually.)*

PEOPLE *(Chanting):* John Henry, John Henry. . . . *(Continuing softly during the following conversation)*

CAPTAIN: John, you've been hammering over eight hours now. You have to stop. The rock's getting harder and harder.

POLLY: Please, John, stop now. You're suffering too much.

JOHN *(Breathlessly, from offstage):* I'm tired. But I won't give up.

PEOPLE *(Chanting louder):* John Henry, John Henry . . .

CAPTAIN *(Worriedly):* John, you don't look well. It's the ninth hour.

POLLY: You've done more than any man could do. Quit now before it's too late.

JOHN *(Groaning):* No! I'll never quit!

PEOPLE *(Chanting loudly):* John Henry, John Henry. . . . *(Sound of train whistle is heard. Sounds of steel striking steel and chugging of steam engine stop, as does the chanting.)*

CAPTAIN: The race is over. The steam drill drove nine feet into the mountain. John Henry drove *(Pauses)* fifteen feet. John Henry wins. (PEOPLE *cheer as* JOHN, *hammer in hand, staggers in, followed by* BILL. CAPTAIN *helps them over to tree stumps;* POLLY *follows, looking worried. Seeing* JOHN's *condition,* PEOPLE *quiet down, whispering nervously among themselves.* JOHN *sinks down on one stump.* BILL *sits on other, wearily holding head in hands.* CAPTAIN *pats* JOHN *on back.)* John, you've won the biggest race of your life. We're all mighty proud of you.

SAM: I never thought a man could do it. He beat my steam drill fair and square. *(Counting out money from pocket)* Captain, here is the five hundred dollars you won from me.

CAPTAIN *(Taking it):* This is your money, John. *(Holds it out to him)* You're the one who earned it. *(JOHN smiles faintly and shakes his head, then looks at exhausted BILL, reaching out to pat his back but not able to reach it. JOHN stands, shakily, reaches out for POLLY, takes a step and collapses. Men gasp, ladies scream, and children run crying to parents. POLLY kneels beside him.)*

POLLY *(Tearfully):* John, why wouldn't you listen to us? *(Touching hammer)* You just kept on hammering *(Voice faltering)* and hammering and—(BILL *rises and helps her to her feet.)*

BILL *(Comforting her):* Polly Anne, a man has to do what he feels is right. *(She nods and wipes away tears.)*

POLLY: Yes, I know. He was doing that.

CAPTAIN: John Henry, as long as there are people like you, there will never be a machine to take the place of a human spirit. *(Looks at money and then at others, helplessly)* I can't keep this money. Polly, you take it. *(She shakes her head and looks away.)* Well, Sam, I guess you'll just have to take it back. *(Hands it to him)* None of us would feel right having it. (SAM *looks at money, then at* JOHN, *and shakes head. He exits with bowed head. Everyone freezes as lights dim. Spotlight goes up on* SINGER, *who enters, playing and singing as before.* PEOPLE, *including* POLLY, BILL *and* CAPTAIN, *join in song.)*

SINGER: Go and tell the story of John Henry,
Born with a hammer that could sing.

PEOPLE: And on hot summer days in the south they say

You can hear his hammer ring.
Lord! Lord!
You can hear his hammer ring.
(Loud sound of steel striking steel is heard, then fades out as lights go out and curtain closes.)

THE END

PRODUCTION NOTES

JOHN HENRY

Characters: 6 male; 3 female; 1 male or female for Ballad Singer (preferably plays guitar); and as many as desired for People (at least 4).

Playing Time: 20 minutes.

Costumes: Typical costume of mid-1800's in the South. Bill and John wear work clothes. Bill also wears cap, bandana around neck, and carries jacket in Scene 1. Polly Anne wears long print dress with apron; she removes apron in Scene 2. Captain Tommy wears vest and visor hat. Sam, a flashy pair of pants with suspenders, and straw hat. Two Women wear fancy long dresses, hats, and carry parasols; Two Men wear suits, carry walking sticks.

Properties: Sledge hammer; pencil and paper; blanket; picnic basket; play money.

Setting: Backdrop painting of countryside in southern United States, with train tracks curving across and appearing to lead off right. At center, two tree stumps can be created from stools covered with brown paper.

Lighting: Spotlight and dimming of lights as indicated in text.

Sound: Train whistle blast; hammer striking steel; chugging steam drill, as indicated in text. Offstage voices may be amplified, if desired.

Harriet Tubman—The Second Moses

by Aileen Fisher

Characters

HARRIET TUBMAN
THREE GIRLS
THREE BOYS
CHORUS *(any number)*

1ST GIRL: When Harriet Tubman
Was six years old
Her childhood was over.
Up till then
She had a carefree life
on the plantation.

HARRIET: The older children were
already working in the fields.
My mother was cook at the Big House.
My father picked cotton or
worked in the piney woods.

2ND GIRL: "Some day," her mother said,
"we will be free.
The master promised me."

HARRIET: I thought very little
about being free.
I thought this was the way
things had to be:
Some people lived in fine houses,
had carriages with horses;
the rest of us lived in cabins
and worked on the plantation,
always in fear of the overseer
who would snap a whip with leather thongs.

1ST BOY: When Harriet turned six,
the master decided she was
strong enough to work for money.
He hired her out to a lady
to take care of her baby
and clean the house.

HARRIET: She was not a kind lady.
She used to whip my legs
when I was slow or
when I looked out of the window.

3RD GIRL: One day Harriet was so tired
she fell asleep rocking the baby.
The lady sent her back to the Big House.
Harriet cried with joy
to be back home again.

CHORUS: *Sings "Swing Low, Sweet Chariot."*

2ND BOY: The master said,
"You're strong for your age.
You'll be a good field hand."

HARRIET: Field work was not easy—
Picking cotton, cotton, cotton all day,
with the sun burning down
sometimes making me dizzy.
But I was glad to be with my people again.
When the overseer could not hear us,
we would talk and sing.

CHORUS: *Sings "My Lord, What a Morning."*

3RD BOY: Often the talk was about freedom,
a word that sounded like music
to Harriet.

HARRIET: By the time I was twelve,
I was handling a plow.
Sometimes when the master
was in need of money,
he rented my father and me out
to work for a neighbor.

1ST BOY: They cut trees,
trimmed off the branches,
and skidded the logs to the loading place.

HARRIET: When I was fifteen,
a black man who was free
came to work on the plantation
for pay.
His name was John Tubman.
We liked to work together.
After a time, John and I
got married. But in a few
months, we were not getting along well.

We didn't agree
on the one great thought
that burned in my heart:
FREEDOM!

CHORUS: *Sings "Go Down, Moses."*

1ST GIRL: John had his papers—
He was already free.
He didn't worry about Harriet
longing for freedom.

HARRIET: Suddenly, life changed again for me.
The master died and
all the slaves on the plantation
worried about what would happen:
Would we get a cruel, new master?
Would we be sold?
Would our families be separated?
The master had promised my mother
her freedom, but he died
before he signed the papers.
What would happen to us?

1ST BOY: They often heard of a
slave escaping from
one of the plantations.
Sometimes a slave would make
his way north to safety.
Sometimes slave-catchers
and their dogs
picked up the trail,
caught him, and

brought him back
to be flogged.

HARRIET: Oh, I knew the dangers,
yet the thought of freedom
was always with me,
glowing like the North Star.
One night, without telling anyone,
I took my brother's shoes
and my father's coat,
put some victuals in a sack,
and headed for the swamp.

CHORUS: *Sings "O, Shenandoah!"*

2ND BOY: Part of Maryland
near Chesapeake Bay
where the plantation lay
was swampy lowland,
with heavy timber and
thick tangles of brush
and rotting logs.

3RD GIRL: Harriet had to push through
this wet, unfriendly country,
away from roads where slave-catchers
might be lurking.
She had to travel by night
with no map to follow,
only the North Star to guide her
to the Promised Land.

HARRIET: If I could get to Philadelphia,

I knew I would be safe.
I was headed for a farm that
welcomed runaway slaves.

CHORUS: *Sings "My Lord, What a Morning."*

3RD BOY: Early on the second morning,
she reached the farm.
She was weary and splattered with mud.
They took her in, fed her, and
gave her dry clothes.
They showed her a place to hide
in the barn under the hay.

HARRIET: They told me where the next
house was on the way
to Philadelphia. "Now you're
on the Underground Railroad,"
they said.

2ND GIRL: The Underground Railroad
was a secret system to
help slaves reach the
free states and Canada.

1ST BOY: One farmer
gave her a ride in his wagon
under a load of corn.
Another farmer, a free black man,
gave her men's clothes to wear.

3RD GIRL: Finally, after many grueling days,
she reached Philadelphia,
where she found refuge

in the home of a Quaker
who ran a "station" on the Underground.
He sent her on to the home
of another Quaker
where she would be safe.

CHORUS: *Sings "Nobody Knows the Trouble I've Seen."*

HARRIET: My new mistress
was kind in every way.
She taught me
the things I should know
about doing housework,
and she paid me in cash.

I saved my money so I could go back south
to rescue my family and friends.
Oh, I knew it was dangerous.
There was a reward posted
for my capture,
a reward of thousands of dollars
for me, dead or alive!

But I knew I had been chosen
to be a second Moses,
to lead my people to freedom.

CHORUS: *Sings "Go Down, Moses."*

HARRIET: "Go down, Moses," I sang my own words.
"Go down, Moses,
Way down in Maryland.
Tell the old masters
to let my people go!"

3RD BOY: In all, Harriet went back south
           nineteen times.
           She led more than three hundred
           of her people
           from slavery to freedom,
           without ever being caught
           or losing a "passenger"
           on the Underground Railroad.

HARRIET: The hardest trip
           was the one I made
           to fetch my old mother and father.
           They were weary and the way
           was long.
           Slave-catchers watched for "Moses"
           at every crossroad.
           We had many narrow escapes.
           But we finally reached
           our promised land—
           the little house I had
           bought in New York state.
           There we found the freedom
           I had dreamed of
           for so long. . . .

CHORUS: *Sings "Swing Low, Sweet Chariot," or any
           other spiritual.*

THE END

Mary McLeod Bethune, Dream Maker

by Mary Satchell

Characters

MARY MCLEOD BETHUNE
BERTHA MITCHELL, *Mary's friend and secretary*
ROSE KEMP, *college freshman*
EMMA WILSON, *Mary's first teacher and mentor*
THOMAS, *student in Mary's first class*
MR. HILL, *Thomas's father*
ALICE JACKSON, *student at Kindell Institute*
REV. WATKINS, *principal of Kindell Institute*
BOY ⎫
⎬ *students in class*
GIRL ⎭
STUDENTS, *six or more, as desired*

SCENE 1

TIME: *1954; Graduation Day and the Fiftieth Anniversary of Bethune-Cookman College.*
SETTING: *Mary Bethune's office at Bethune-Cookman College in Daytona Beach, Florida. Desk and chair are placed downstage, center. A phone, letter opener, and two or three stacks of mail are on desk. At left is a*

small bookcase filled with books. Two chairs are op-
posite desk, a small table is near exit at right.

AT RISE: MARY BETHUNE *sits at desk, opening and*
reading telegrams and letters. BERTHA MITCHELL *en-*
ters, carrying maroon cap and gown, and pauses near
table.

BERTHA *(Scolding mildly):* Why, Mary Bethune, how
can you work at a time like this? The graduation exer-
cises will begin in little more than an hour. *(Places cap*
and gown on table) The seniors are already lining up in
front of the auditorium.

MARY *(Continuing to open mail):* This isn't work,
Bertha. I'm having the time of my life reading these
beautiful messages from my friends all over the world.
It's hard to believe that we've been running this college for 50 years.

BERTHA *(Coming to stand near desk):* We're going to
have lovely weather for today's graduation. There's not
a cloud in sight.

MARY *(Putting down letter opener):* I gave some thought
to having this year's program outside, but then I remembered what happened on our thirty-fifth anniversary.

BERTHA: Wasn't that the year Mrs. Eleanor Roosevelt
came down to be our guest speaker?

MARY *(Nodding and leaning back in her chair):* How
could I forget! We had hundreds of chairs set up on the
campus lawn, and the moment Mrs. Roosevelt stood
up to speak, it started raining.

BERTHA: What *I'll* never forget is how you walked to
Mrs. Roosevelt's side and held an umbrella over her
head while she gave her entire address.

MARY *(Mischievously):* She didn't see me glaring at the
audience, daring them to move from their seats. *(She*
and BERTHA *laugh.)*

BERTHA: I can laugh about that rainy graduation day now, but I certainly didn't feel like laughing then.

MARY *(Reminiscing):* I was thinking back to the year you started working as my secretary. Booker T. Washington paid his first visit to our school that same year. It was in 1908.

BERTHA *(Sitting in chair):* I remember it very well, Mary.

MARY: I'm afraid you didn't have much faith in me or my dreams in those days. *(Chuckling)* You were embarrassed because we had only one building to show Mr. Washington.

BERTHA *(Laughing at herself):* And that wasn't even finished. *(With broad sweep of her arm)* If only Mr. Washington could see it today: a four-year college with nineteen buildings! (ROSE KEMP *appears at exit, hesitates.*)

MARY *(Motioning* ROSE *to enter):* Don't stand there looking as if you're meeting the enemy, young lady. Everyone's welcome here. (ROSE *enters, appearing uncomfortable as she clutches a notepad.*)

ROSE *(Hesitantly):* Mrs. Bethune, my name is Rose Kemp, and I'd like to interview you this afternoon, if I may.

MARY *(Amused):* Who sent you, Rose? From the look on your face, you didn't come here on your own.

ROSE *(Eagerly):* I volunteered for this assignment, Mrs. Bethune. You see, I'm a freshman, and I want to make the campus newspaper staff, but the editor says I don't have what it takes to be a reporter.

MARY *(Indignantly):* I'm glad you didn't let yourself be discouraged by that kind of talk.

ROSE: I thought if I could get an interview with you, the editor might change his mind.

BERTHA *(Standing up):* Excuse me, Mrs. Bethune, but

in a little while you'll have to start greeting your
guests.

MARY: Surely we can make time for something as important as a young student's future. (*Smiles at* ROSE) I
think Rose and I may have a lot in common. We both
have the spirit to show others what we can do.

BERTHA *(Reluctantly):* Very well. Only fifteen or
twenty minutes, though, please, Mrs. Bethune, or
your entire schedule will be ruined.

MARY: Much can be done in fifteen minutes. *(Kindly)*
Now, Rose, if you keep your questions short and to the
point, I'm sure we'll both make our deadlines.

BERTHA *(Resigned):* I should have known better than to
say anything. You've never refused to give any student
your time.

MARY: This is what I've lived and worked for all these
years, Bertha. I can't stop now. (BERTHA *exits. To*
ROSE, *humorously*) I can always tell when my assistant is annoyed with me. She calls me *Mrs. Bethune.* (ROSE *laughs and relaxes.*) Sit down, Rose, and
ask whatever you wish. I'm always ready to talk.
(ROSE *sits on edge of chair and holds her pen poised
over pad.*)

ROSE: How did you get started as a teacher, Mrs. Bethune?

MARY: That question could take all day to answer. I
didn't want to be a teacher, not at first.

ROSE *(Surprised and interested):* Really? What did you
want to be?

MARY: I wanted to be a missionary, Rose. And do you
know, I think I got my heart's desire. *(With mounting
excitement)* Let me tell you something of my adventure, Rose. And we won't worry about the time, just
now. (ROSE *begins to write, as curtain closes.*)

*   *   *   *   *

SCENE 2

TIME: *1896.*

SETTING: *The Presbyterian Mission School in Mayes-ville, South Carolina. At center, teacher's desk and chair face a long, wooden table—with several books and old-fashioned writing slate on it—and a bench with a student's jacket lying on it. Paper, pen and globe are on desk. Exit is right.*

AT RISE: MARY *tidies schoolroom. She stacks a few books from table on her desk, then goes back to bench and picks up jacket.* EMMA WILSON *comes into doorway, and seeing* MARY, *enters.*

EMMA *(Lightly):* Mary McLeod, when will you stop working and go home? Don't you ever get tired of this place?

MARY *(Surprised):* Tired of school? Good heavens, no! *(Looks around with pleasure)* This is where I come whenever I'm weary and need to be refreshed. Teaching never tires me, Miss Wilson. *(Hangs jacket over back of her chair)*

EMMA *(Laughing):* Mary, you remind me so much of myself when I started teaching. Such enthusiasm and excitement! When you first walked into my classroom so many years ago, I knew instinctively you were going to be my best student.

MARY: You had such confidence in me, Miss Wilson; I just had to live up to your expectations.

EMMA *(Becoming thoughtful, then seriously):* Mary, you've done such wonderful things for the children in this community. I've taught here in Mayesville for a long time, and I've never been as close to these youngsters as you've become in a single year.

MARY: Thank you, Miss Wilson. Your opinion of my work is very important to me.

EMMA: I know that, Mary. *(Hesitating)* And I . . . I don't want you to be discouraged by some of the gossip you may soon hear.

MARY *(Puzzled):* What gossip, Miss Wilson?

EMMA *(Forcing a smile):* I'm sure it's nothing, dear. You see, I've grown into something of a worrywart over the years, but this little community is set in its ways.

MARY *(Shaking head):* You don't have to remind me of that, Miss Wilson. I was born and raised here.

EMMA: Of course, you understand the people well, Mary. Probably better than I ever will. *(Voice borders on anger.)* But there's just no pleasing some folk!

MARY *(Sitting at desk):* Miss Wilson, I sense that you're trying to tell me something. Have I done anything wrong?

EMMA *(Laughing harshly):* Oh, Mary, no. *(Moves quickly to desk, and stands in front of it)* Why, my dear, you're just about the best thing that's ever happened to this place. You're a young, bright teacher who loves and understands these children.

MARY: Then what is it? What's gone wrong?

EMMA *(Pausing):* Some parents are complaining that you're putting new-fangled ideas in their children's heads. (MARY *remains quietly attentive.*) Many children don't want to stay and work on the farm any more. Since you've become their teacher, they talk about getting more schooling and, perhaps, leaving town.

MARY: What's wrong with that? *(Touching globe)* I've told my students this is a big world, and Mayesville is only a very tiny part of it. I want my children to know they can earn a good place for themselves in this world.

EMMA: I understand that, Mary, but some of their parents are afraid of your ideas. They don't have the faith in their children that you do.

MARY *(Rising; with determination):* I believe my students can be anything they want to be, Miss Wilson. And I will not rest till they believe it, too.

EMMA *(Gently):* I know, Mary, but sometimes we may have to bend a little in order to get the results we want. *(Touches* MARY's *shoulder)* You're still very young and idealistic.

MARY *(Firmly):* I know in my heart that I'm right, Miss Wilson, no matter what others may think.

EMMA *(Sighing):* We'll be thankful for Mary McLeod one day, for sure. *(Knock at door is heard.)*

MARY: Come in. (THOMAS *enters shyly and takes off cap.)*

THOMAS: I'm sorry to bother you, Miss McLeod, but I forgot my jacket.

MARY *(Cheerfully):* Why, Thomas, I was going to bring you your jacket this afternoon. *(Hands jacket to* THOMAS)

THOMAS *(Embarrassed):* I don't think you should stop by my house, Miss McLeod. My papa may not make you feel welcome.

EMMA *(Moving closer to* THOMAS): Is your father at home now?

THOMAS: I don't know, Miss Wilson. I turned around and came back for my jacket before I got home. Papa usually won't stop working until dinnertime.

EMMA: Your father works very hard, Thomas. And he's a good father.

THOMAS: I know that, Miss Wilson. *(Dejectedly)* Sometimes, though, I wish he could understand . . .

MARY: Understand what, Thomas?

THOMAS *(Frowning):* Papa wants me to be a farmer, but

I want to be a doctor. He says I'm just dreaming of things that can never come true.

MARY: And I say your dreams can and *will* come true, Thomas, if you're willing to work hard enough.

THOMAS *(Bewildered):* But, Miss McLeod, you say one thing, and my papa says another. How can I tell who's right?

EMMA *(Kindly):* Thomas, you must follow your own heart whenever you have to make a hard decision.

THOMAS: Then I'll become a doctor.

MARY *(Smiling):* You have the ability to be an excellent doctor. (MR. HILL *strides through doorway, startling everyone.* THOMAS *looks apprehensively at his father.* MARY *tries to be friendly.)* Good afternoon, Mr. Hill.

MR. HILL *(Gruffly):* I didn't come to pay a social call, Miss McLeod. *(To* THOMAS) I knew you'd be here. Why didn't you come straight home as I told you? We've got a lot of work to do.

MARY: Thomas left his jacket, Mr. Hill, and came back to get it. Please don't be angry with him.

MR. HILL *(Ignoring her):* Tom, go on home now. I'll be there in a minute.

THOMAS: Yes, sir. *(Exits quickly)*

MR. HILL *(Scowling at* MARY): I resent your putting all those useless notions in my son's head. Instead of working on the farm, he wants to become a doctor!

EMMA: Mr. Hill, I think you're being unfair to Miss McLeod.

MR. HILL: I knew Mary McLeod's parents before she was born. They're not ashamed to be farmers.

MARY *(Struggling for patience):* I'm proud of what my parents have achieved, and they *encouraged* me to go to school and be a teacher.

MR. HILL (*Stubbornly*): Maybe Sam McLeod let his daughter have her way, but my son's going to be a farmer, and that's final!

MARY: Mr. Hill, is it fair to force your child to be something he doesn't want to be?

MR. HILL (*Pointing a finger at* MARY): I'm a lot older than you, young lady, and I've raised five children besides Thomas. I've got more experience than you in these matters.

MARY (*Resolutely*): Your son has an excellent mind. He wants to use his mind to the best of his ability.

MR. HILL: This is 1896, Mary McLeod, and a black youngster can break his heart fighting against the odds. (*Voice softens*) You may not think so, but I love my son, and I don't want to see him hurt.

EMMA: It seems you both want what's best for Thomas. At least, that's a starting point.

MR. HILL: I've got no quarrel with you, Miss Wilson. You've been the kind of teacher that Mayesville can be proud of. We need more teachers like you, and fewer troublemakers. (*Casts angry look at* MARY)

EMMA (*In a low, steady voice*): Miss McLeod is a very good teacher. In fact, I intend to recommend that she take my place as permanent teacher when I retire. (MARY, *stunned, goes to sit at her desk, and busies herself with papers.* THOMAS *suddenly re-appears at door.*)

MR. HILL (*Abruptly*): What are you doing here, Tom? (THOMAS, *holding his cap tightly, walks to his father.*)

THOMAS (*Quietly*): I've got something to tell you, Papa.

MR. HILL: It can wait, son. Your mother will be needing your help at home.

THOMAS (*Determined*): I have to tell you now. (MARY,

concerned, stands up.)

MARY *(Quickly breaking in):* Is there anything I can do, Thomas?

THOMAS: No, Miss McLeod. I've made up my mind to quit school right away. *(Adults look stunned.)*

MR. HILL *(Angrily):* What kind of foolish talk is that? You can't stop going to school. I won't hear of it.

THOMAS *(Confused):* But, you said you didn't want me to go to school.

MR. HILL *(Impatiently):* I said no such thing. I want you to be a farmer, and farmers need to know as much as they can. They have to run a business.

THOMAS *(Tearfully):* It seems I can never please you, no matter how hard I try. *(Shoulders sag, sighs dejectedly)* All right, Papa, I'll do as you say, but don't blame Miss McLeod. She only tried to help. *(Head down,* THOMAS *moves slowly right.)*

MR. HILL *(Starting after* TOM): Tom, son, wait— (THOMAS *exits without looking back.* MR. HILL *looks at others in bewilderment.)* I never saw my boy look so hurt before. All his spirit seems to be gone.

EMMA: Maybe I can talk to him. *(Exits hurriedly)*

MR. HILL *(Glancing anxiously at* MARY): I didn't mean to do this to him. *(Sits on bench worriedly)*

MARY *(Earnestly):* Mr. Hill, how many of your children are still living at home?

MR. HILL: Three. Tom is the youngest and the smartest, I have to admit.

MARY: Our little school can hold only so many students, and most families in Mayesville are quite large. I plan to ask the parents to let me teach their youngest children year round.

MR. HILL *(Thinking it over; slowly):* Only the youngest?

MARY: I'll promise to let the others work the farms, and

maybe someday we'll have a school big enough for all the children.

MR. HILL: You're one smart lady, Miss McLeod. I guess I can't refuse your offer, since we'll be left with two kids to help out when Tom's in school.

MARY: I'll certainly be back to get your other two, but that will take a while. (*They laugh.* MR. HILL *rises.*)

MR. HILL: I apologize, Miss McLeod. Emma Wilson was right. You *are* a good teacher. You do care about these kids, and I'm going to see to it that all my neighbors find out what you're doing for us.

MARY: And what about your boy's future?

MR. HILL (*Sincerely*): Miss McLeod, you've convinced me that my son should get all the schooling he can. (*Pausing*) If he wants to be a doctor, I think he ought to have the chance.

MARY (*Gratefully*): Thank you, Mr. Hill. (*Puts out her hand*) I know Thomas will make you very proud. (*They shake hands.*)

MR. HILL: Good day, ma'am. (*Puts on hat, exits.* MARY *stands thoughtfully for a moment, then returns to desk and absently studies the globe.* EMMA *enters, excitedly.*)

EMMA: Mary McLeod, how on earth did you perform this miracle? Mr. Hill is a changed man! And I never saw a happier child than Tom when his father told him he could try to be a doctor. (*Goes to* MARY; *solemnly*) How do you feel about teaching here permanently? You know I must retire soon.

MARY: Thank you for your confidence in me, Miss Wilson, but I can't spend the rest of my life in Mayesville.

EMMA (*Greatly disappointed*): Why, Mary, has all this talk made you want to leave us?

MARY: No, that had nothing to do with my decision, Miss Wilson. I guess I've always known, deep down, that I'd have to move on someday.

EMMA: Are you sure you're not making a mistake, Mary?

MARY: I don't know. I only know that something is pulling me toward my destiny.

EMMA *(Sadly):* How soon do you plan to leave? *(Quietly)* And how will we tell Thomas?

MARY: I'll stay here and teach for a few more years. Thomas will be all right.

EMMA *(With concern):* Mary, where will you go?

MARY *(Confidently):* I don't know yet what I'm to do with my life, but one thing I'm sure of, I *must* keep searching until I find out. *(Curtain)*

* * * * *

SCENE 3

TIME: *A few years later.*

SETTING: *Classroom at Kindell Institute in Sumter, South Carolina. Mary McLeod Bethune's desk and chair are up left, opposite two or three rows of her students' old-fashioned desks. A wastebasket and lectern stand beside Mary's desk, which has books and globe on it. Exit is right.*

AT RISE: ALICE JACKSON *somberly enters, carrying books, which she puts inside her desk. She goes to* MARY's *desk and plays with the globe absently, slowly spinning it as she leans against the desk.* MARY *enters unnoticed, and studies the girl before speaking.*

MARY *(Brightly):* Why, Alice, you're certainly the early bird today. The rest of your family must still be at the breakfast table. *(Takes off shawl and drapes it over back of her chair)*

ALICE *(Glancing curiously at* MARY): I don't have a family, Mrs. Bethune. My parents died a long time ago. I live at the Children's Home.

MARY *(Sadly):* Goodness, you're only a young girl, and you talk as if you're older than I am.

ALICE: But it's true. *(Sadly)* I wish I did have a family like the other children here at school.

MARY *(Putting hand on* ALICE's *shoulder):* Alice, I think you should count your blessings. Why, you're far more fortunate than many of your classmates.

ALICE *(Shaking head):* How can you say that, Mrs. Bethune?

MARY: You have a very large family at the Children's Home. There are people at that orphanage who love and care for you just as parents do. If you look at it that way, every boy and girl at the Children's Home is really your brother and sister.

ALICE: I hadn't thought of it like that. (ALICE *turns back to globe and spins it.)*

MARY: That globe was given to me when I graduated from Scotia Seminary years ago. *(Enthusiastically)* I've kept it since as a reminder of how big and wonderful this world is.

ALICE *(Mockingly):* It looks very tiny to me, Mrs. Bethune. *(Puts finger on one spot of globe)* See? I can cover up a whole island with just one of my fingers.

MARY *(Amused):* You know this globe is only on a very small scale, Alice. Of course, we all know that in reality, our world is extremely large, and you mustn't forget it. Never limit your future or your dreams.

ALICE *(Moving from desk):* Mrs. Bethune, I used to

dream of being adopted and having a mother and father of my own. *(Wistfully)* We would live in our own house; I'd have clothes as nice as the other girls at school. I waited a long time for someone to come to the orphanage and take me home. *(Looks down at her shoes)* But nobody ever came.

MARY *(Putting her arm around* ALICE's *shoulder):* Perhaps you should change your dream a little. *I* did, when I was about twenty years old. You see, I didn't really want to be a schoolteacher.

ALICE *(Shyly):* You're the best teacher I ever had, Mrs. Bethune.

MARY: When I hear one of my students say that, I'm glad I had to change my dream of being a missionary. Teachers get the chance to help so many people.

ALICE *(Shyly):* I hope someday I can help a lot of people. *(Other students enter, carrying books. They greet* MARY, *take seats, and put books in desks.* ALICE *goes to her seat.* MARY *goes to her desk and sits.)*

MARY *(Cheerfully):* Good morning, everyone. We're going to begin our class a little differently today. I'd like you to talk about your secret dreams—what you would *really* like to be when you grow up. Who wants to start? *(Silence. Finally,* BOY *raises his hand.)* Yes?

BOY: I want to be a preacher like our principal, Reverend Watkins.

GIRL *(Smirking):* Humph! You're too bad to be a minister. *(All laugh.)*

MARY *(Reproachfully):* I don't want to hear any more of that. *(Glances casually at class, then lets her eyes rest on* ALICE) Alice, what's your secret dream?

ALICE *(Caught offguard):* Well . . . *(Very softly)* I want to be a nurse.

STUDENTS *(From opposite side of the class; ad lib):* Talk
louder, Alice. We can't hear you. *(Etc.)*

ALICE *(Loudly and defiantly):* I want to be a nurse.

MARY *(Gently, firmly):* Then it's settled, Alice. That's
what you will be.

ALICE: But I live at the Children's Home, Mrs. Bethune.
How could I ever get to nursing school?

MARY *(Decisively, leaving her desk):* We'll talk about
that as soon as I get back. Excuse me for a moment,
class. *(Exits rapidly)*

BOY *(Threateningly, turning to* GIRL): So I'm too bad to
be a preacher, am I? *(He gets a slingshot from his
desk.)*

STUDENTS *(Ad lib):* I dare you. Leave her alone! *(Etc.)*

GIRL *(Fearfully):* You'd better not do that! I'll tell Mrs.
Bethune! (MARY *re-enters, briskly;* BOY *quickly hides
slingshot.* REV. WATKINS *enters, follows* MARY *to her
desk. Class quickly quiets down.)*

MARY *(Standing behind desk):* Class, I asked Reverend
Watkins to tell you a little about his life, especially his
youth. *(To* REV. WATKINS) Reverend, we'd like to hear
about your childhood, and how you came to be a school
principal. *(Sits at desk)*

WATKINS *(Standing at lectern; to* MARY): Thank you,
Mrs. Bethune. *(To class)* Good morning, boys and
girls. *(Gives a little bow)*

STUDENTS *(Together):* Good morning, Reverend
Watkins.

WATKINS: I didn't expect to be making a speech so early,
but I'm always glad to talk to our students. *(Takes off
glasses, wipes them with handkerchief, then puts them
on again)* Mrs. Bethune tells me you've been talking
about your plans for the future. My future seemed

pretty dismal when I was your age. *(Sighs)* You see, I was an orphan, and I lived at the Children's Home right here in town. (ALICE, *shocked, leans forward.*) But I wanted to be something in life, to get an education, and to help others.

ALICE: You must have been adopted by rich people who could send you away to college.

WATKINS *(Smiling):* That was my secret dream for over twelve years, Alice. However, nobody ever came to adopt me, either rich or poor. I stayed at the Children's Home till I was old enough to go out on my own. I took any job I could get to finish college.

ALICE *(With awe):* You came from the Children's Home, Reverend Watkins, and yet your dreams came true?

WATKINS *(Assertively):* I *made* my dreams come true, young lady, and so can all of you.

MARY *(Graciously):* Thank you. You've been a great help to us, Reverend Watkins.

WATKINS: Please invite me again, and next time, I'll spend more time with you. *(Bowing to* MARY*)* And before I go, I think the class would like to ask you about *your* secret dream, Mrs. Bethune. *(Turns to class)* Isn't that right? *(Students nod their heads and clap their hands.)*

MARY *(Flustered):* I didn't expect the tables to be turned this way. *(Laughs lightly)* Yet I suppose it's only fair.

BOY: Mrs. Bethune, I'll bet you want to be a principal like Rev. Watkins.

MARY: You're getting warm, but not quite. What I really want to do is establish a college one day. My son Albert, Jr. is just an infant, but I want to see him in a good college when he's old enough. And I want to see every other youngster get the same opportunity.

WATKINS *(Sincerely):* I have no doubt that you will build your college, Mrs. Bethune. It's just a matter of time. My only regret is that you'll be leaving us someday.

MARY: My husband said there may be some opportunity for us in Florida. A new railroad's being built on the east coast of the state, and we plan to visit there soon.

WATKINS: I wish you well, Mrs. Bethune. Some of my friends live in Daytona Beach. I hope you'll find time to look them up.

MARY: It will be my pleasure, Reverend Watkins. *(With fervor)* Wherever my journey may lead me, I'm sure I'll spend the rest of my days in helping students like these to have happier and better lives. *(Curtain)*

*   *   *   *   *

EPILOGUE

TIME: *1954.*

SETTING: *Same as in Scene 1.*

AT RISE: MARY *sits, holding mortarboard and graduation robe.* ROSE *holds notepad.*

MARY: So then, Rose, my family and I moved here to Daytona Beach, and I opened my tiny school in 1904. (ROSE *jots down some notes.*) There were only five students at the time. In 1923, my school for girls was combined with a boys' school, Cookman Institute of Jacksonville.

ROSE *(Proudly):* And now Bethune-Cookman College has over 1,300 students.

MARY *(Smiling radiantly):* Yes. So you see, Rose, my life has been a grand adventure, and I honestly can say that it still is an adventure.

ROSE *(Scribbling rapidly on notepad):* That's a beautiful quote to end my feature article with, Mrs. Bethune.

(With great enthusiasm) This is going to be one of the best stories ever printed in our college newspaper.

MARY: I'm eager to read it. (*Shakes a finger at* ROSE) Just you be sure to quote me correctly and get all the facts straight.

ROSE: Oh, I will! I can't afford to make any mistakes. It will give me the chance I need. My career in journalism may depend on how this article turns out.

MARY: Nonsense, your career *and* your future would hardly depend on one little incident. What you become depends largely on what you *do*, hour after hour, day after day, year after year. (MARY *picks up robe.*)

ROSE: Please let me help you with that, Mrs. Bethune. (*Helps* MARY *put on robe*)

MARY: Thank you, my dear. (*Facing* ROSE) Now that we have only a few moments left together, I'll ask you a question, Rose. You've asked me so many.

ROSE (*Flippantly*): Fire away!

MARY: Just what is your secret dream?

ROSE (*A bit defensively*): Why would you want to know that, Mrs. Bethune?

MARY: I always get around to asking that of every young person I meet. Give me an answer quickly. (BERTHA *enters right.*)

BERTHA (*Anxiously*): The program's about to begin. All the seniors are in line and ready to march into the auditorium. Please hurry, Mary. Everyone's waiting for you.

MARY: I'll be there in a moment, Bertha. (BERTHA *exits, and* "Pomp *and* Circumstance" *begins to play softly offstage.*)

ROSE (*Evasively*): We don't have time to talk any longer, Mrs. Bethune. The music has started.

MARY *(Persistently):* Oh yes, we do, Rose. I won't budge until you tell me.

ROSE *(Relenting):* All right. I really dream of publishing my own weekly newspaper.

MARY: Promise me you won't stop until you reach your goal.

ROSE *(Vowing solemnly):* I promise that, one day, I'll have my own newspaper. *(Strains of graduation music grow louder.)*

MARY *(Adjusting mortarboard):* Now, it's time to go. We'll meet again at this same place three years from today, Rose. I'll present you the college newspaper editor's award at your graduation. Is that a deal?

ROSE *(Happily):* Yes, Mrs. Bethune. It's a deal! *(They exit. MARY, with head high, leads the way. Music grows louder, and continues to end of march. Curtain)*

THE END

PRODUCTION NOTES

MARY McLEOD BETHUNE: DREAM MAKER

Characters: 4 male; 6 female. Six or more additional boys and girls for classroom scene.

Playing Time: 30 minutes.

Costumes: Scene 1: Mary Bethune is a dignified older woman with gray hair. She wears conservative jacket dress and single strand of pearls. Bertha and Rose wear clothes appropriate for the mid 1950s. Scene 2: Traditional late 19th century dress. Women may wear long-sleeved blouses and ankle-length skirts. Mary is a young woman. Emma's hair is graying. Thomas and Mr. Hill wear farmer's clothes. Mr. Hill wears battered wide-brimmed hat, and Thomas has a cap and jacket. Scene 3: Alice wears a faded calico or homespun-type dress. Mary wears short cape or shawl. Reverend Watkins wears dark suit with frock coat and high collared shirt, and glasses.

Properties: Cap and gown, notepad, pen, papers, books, glasses, handkerchief, slingshot.

Setting: Scene 1: Mary Bethune's office. Mary's desk and chair are down center. A phone, letter opener and two or three stacks of mail are on desk. At left is a small bookcase filled with books. Two chairs are opposite desk, and small table is near exit at right. Scene 2: A little rural schoolroom. A teacher's desk and chair face a long wooden table and bench. Some books, and an old-fashioned writing slate are on table. Paper, pen and a globe of the earth are on desk. Exit is right. Scene 3: Larger classroom. Mary's desk and chair are upstage left, opposite two or three rows of old-fashioned desks. A wastebasket and lectern stand beside desk, which holds a few books supported by bookends and the globe. Exit is right. Epilogue: Same as Scene 1.

Sound: Graduation music, as indicated in text.

Abe Lincoln and the Runaways

by *Wenta Jean Watson*

Characters

CALLIE ⎫
BIG JIM ⎭ *runaway slaves*
MR. TANDY
JUDGE ROLLINS
ABE LINCOLN
HIRAM
TEACHER
LEE
MATILDA
ELIZA
PHOEBE

TIME: *Early fall, 1822.*

BEFORE RISE: BIG JIM *and* CALLIE, *carrying sack, run in from right. They stop and look around cautiously.*

CALLIE: I'm tired, Big Jim. We just can't outrun them.

BIG JIM: Callie, we came a long way from that plantation. I don't know what's ahead, but I have a dream of living free and of raising my children free, and if I have to run till I drop, then that's the way it's going to be!

CALLIE *(Looking off right):* I hear them coming. Where are we going to hide?

BIG JIM (*Looking around, then pointing off left*): Behind that rock. Hurry. (*He takes her hand, and they exit left.* MR. TANDY *and* JUDGE ROLLINS *enter from right, carrying riding crops.*)

JUDGE: They have to be near here. They can't get any farther on foot.

MR. TANDY: There's a search party out looking for them now, Judge Rollins. They'll find your slaves soon.

JUDGE: They'd better. I have to leave tomorrow. My ship for France sails next week. I'll give the searchers double what I offered them. If those slaves get away, others will try to escape, too.

MR. TANDY: With double reward money I can assure you that the runaways will be found.

JUDGE: I hate to lose them. Big Jim is a good worker, and his sister Callie is the best cook I've ever had. (*Rubs his stomach*) If we find them in time, Callie can fix a good meal for me before I have to leave. (*They exit left. After a few moments,* BIG JIM *and* CALLIE *enter from left, look around cautiously.*)

BIG JIM (*Wiping his brow*): That was a close call.

CALLIE (*Taking two apples out of sack, and handing one to* BIG JIM): We ought to eat something.

BIG JIM: All right, but we have to keep moving while we eat. No time to stop. (*They start off left.*)

CALLIE: Where are we going to hide till dark?

BIG JIM: From up on the hill I spied a schoolhouse. After the children go home, we'll get in through an open window and stay there. There won't be anybody around.

CALLIE: It will be good to rest, and a school will be safe.

BIG JIM: I hope so, Callie. But we can't even trust a child—catching runaways means money, you know. Let's go. (*They exit left.*)

* * * * *

SETTING: *Indiana. Log cabin schoolhouse with steps and working door is center. Large window is on right side of house; bench stands near it. Several logs of various sizes are scattered around in front of bench.*

AT RISE: ABE *is seated on one step; facing him on another step is* HIRAM. *Both are reading books.* ABE *is mumbling the words out loud.* BIG JIM *sneaks in right, unnoticed by* ABE *and* HIRAM, *and crosses to bench. He places bench beneath window, climbs up on it and peers inside schoolhouse, then ducks down and waits.*

HIRAM: Abe . . . *(There is no answer.)* Abraham! . . . *(Still no response)* Abraham!!

ABE *(Looking up):* Yes, Hiram?

HIRAM: I wish you wouldn't read out loud.

ABE: I like to listen to the sound of the words. Seems I can remember them better if I speak them. (TEACHER *comes out of schoolhouse door and looks at boys.* ABE *continues to read out loud.* BIG JIM *peers in through window again and then motions offstage to* CALLIE, *who enters.* BIG JIM *climbs into school through window and leans out to help* CALLIE. *She drops sack on ground, gives one hand to* BIG JIM *and holds her skirt up with other. After they are inside, she leans out to get sack, but* BIG JIM *pulls her back quickly.*)

TEACHER *(To* ABE): Are you both going to stay here, Abe?

ABE: Sir, I thought I would do some reading in *Pilgrim's Progress* before I go home. I have lots of chores to do before bedtime, and it's hard to read by lamp light.

HIRAM: I don't do chores. When I get home, I go straight to the stables to look at that big bay Pa bought at the auction last month. We plan to race him and make lots of money.

TEACHER: I'm proud of both of you.

ABE: Ma sets great store by learning and tells me to keep at it.

TEACHER: It's the key to the world.

ABE: I've seen some educated fellers that don't impress me much. I'd say they were educated fools.

TEACHER *(Pointing to heart):* It's what's in here that counts. But you have to use your head along with it. *(Pauses)* Our nation is growing all the time. People are pushing West every day. There will be new states joining the Union and opportunities for educated men to represent them in Washington. You keep on with the studying, and someday you might be two of the men responsible for decision-making in this country.

HIRAM: Do you suppose slavery will be allowed in the West? There is a great deal of talk for and against it.

TEACHER: I don't know. There is much dissension over the question throughout the land. The North generally opposes it, but the economy of the South is built on slavery.

ABE: I don't think it's right for one man to own another, as if he were property.

HIRAM: I wager that if your father had the money he would buy a field hand.

ABE: I don't think so. Pa had trouble with land deeds in Kentucky, but I think one reason we moved here to Indiana was to get away from slavery.

TEACHER: Someday the disagreement over slavery may come close to tearing our Union apart.

HIRAM: What do you mean?

TEACHER: War may eventually have to settle the issue. I hate to think of it. If the North and South clash, it will take a giant of a man to lead the country and to keep it together.

HIRAM: I'd like to be that man. Father and Mother say

I'm destined to be in high places. They say it's because of the extra study I do here at school.

TEACHER: You and Abe are good students. In a few years we'll see how you both turn out. *(Pause)* Would one of you bring in some firewood before you go home?

HIRAM: Certainly. *(Gets up and places hands on back)* Oh-h, I just remembered my back—I hurt it yesterday while I was out riding. Abe can fetch the wood.

ABE *(Standing up and closing book):* I'll get it now, sir.

TEACHER: Thank you, Abe. I'll see you tomorrow. *(He exits left. As ABE puts down his book, LEE enters right, carrying a fish pole made of tree branch.)*

LEE: Hi, fellas. I'm going fishing. Come along.

ABE: I can't go, Lee. I have to get some wood for the school, and then I want to do some more reading.

LEE: Just tie the fishing line around your toe, and you can keep on with your everlasting reading, Abe.

ABE *(Shaking head):* Some other time, Lee.

LEE: How about you, Hiram?

HIRAM: No. Fishing's messy business. All those wiggly worms! Not to mention cleaning the fish. But, if you catch any big ones, Father will buy them from you— that is, *if* you will clean them first.

LEE: Sorry, Hiram. Whatever I catch, I clean and eat. *(He starts to exit, then turns back.)* Say, I hear there's a party of men out looking for some runaway slaves.

HIRAM *(Excitedly):* Maybe there's a reward out!

ABE: Would you turn them in for money?

HIRAM *(Stiffly):* Yes, I would. I believe in keeping the law. Slaves are considered property and should be returned to their owner.

ABE: But they're not property. They're people like us.

LEE *(Laughing):* Hiram, I can see the shingle hanging outside your law office in a few years. *(Points to imagi-*

nary sign) Hiram Scarem, Attorney-at-law. *(He laughs again and then sobers as he looks offstage.)* Uh-oh. Have to go, friends. I see the girls headed this way, and I don't want to be cornered by them. *(He exits left. From offstage right are heard sounds of laughter.)*

GIRLS *(Ad lib; calling from offstage):* Lee! You can't run away from us! *(Etc.* HIRAM *smooths his hair and sits back, while* ABE *gathers wood.* MATILDA, ELIZA, *and* PHOEBE *enter from right and start playing a game of tag.* ABE *sees sack on ground, puts down wood and looks in sack, pulls out apple, looks up at window, puts apple back, and then tosses sack inside window. He picks up wood and crosses to girls, who join hands and dance around* ABE. *As they dance, they begin chanting together.)* We're going to have a party! We're going to have a party!

MATILDA *(Dropping hands of other girls):* Eliza is going to have a candypulling Saturday night, Abe. You will come, won't you?

ABE: Thank you, Matilda, but I had my mind set on studying.

ELIZA: We won't let you escape till you say "yes." *(Girls again join hands and begin to dance around him.)*

PHOEBE: Uncle Jess is going to play his banjo for us. We'll have a dance later.

ABE *(Turning around in circle):* I'm not good at dancing, but I do like candy. I'll try to come. *(Girls unclasp hands, allowing* ABE *to take wood into schoolhouse.)*

MATILDA: Hiram, will you come?

HIRAM: I planned to pay a call on my grandmother.

ELIZA: Too bad, because my cousin Jane will be there. Her father is a Congressman.

HIRAM: A Congressman, you say? Hm-m-m. Perhaps I

could talk my brother into visiting Grandma. I wouldn't want to disappoint a charming young lady like you. (*He bows deeply to* ELIZA.)

ELIZA (*Looking off right*): Who are those men riding up?

MATILDA (*Also looking off*): I think it is Judge Rollins and his overseer. (JUDGE ROLLINS *and* MR. TANDY *enter from right.*)

JUDGE: Hello, children. Did you just get out of school?

PHOEBE: Yes, sir.

JUDGE: Some of you may know me. I'm Judge Rollins, and this is my overseer, Mr. Tandy. We are visiting in the neighborhood.

HIRAM: How do you do? (*Looks off right*) Sir, you have mighty fine-looking horses.

JUDGE: Finest this side of the Ohio River, son.

MR. TANDY: Sir, perhaps these children have seen the runaways. (ABE *comes to door and listens.*)

JUDGE: Could be, Mr. Tandy. (*To children*) Two of my slaves have run off, a sister and brother. Their names are Callie and Big Jim. Has any of you seen them?

GIRLS (*Ad lib*): No. Haven't seen them. (*Etc.*)

MR. TANDY: How about you boys?

HIRAM: We've heard about them.

ABE: Have they done anyone harm, or stolen anything?

JUDGE: No, they just up and ran off. They're my property—I pay tax on them, and I want them back.

ABE: They must have had cause to run away.

MR. TANDY: Nonsense! They want to be free—that's all.

ABE: Can't say I blame them. I wouldn't want to be owned, the same as an animal. (*He looks at* HIRAM.) I hear some people treat their thoroughbreds better than their slaves. (*He comes down steps.*)

HIRAM: That's not important, Abe. Slaves are property, pure and simple.

JUDGE *(Impatiently):* Come, come. Have you seen them?

HIRAM: Are you offering a good reward?

MR. TANDY *(Sharply):* Look here. Do you know anything about them or not?

HIRAM *(Slyly):* I sure do love good horseflesh.

JUDGE: Young man, are you trying to blackmail me out of my horses?

HIRAM: No. But if I had a horse like yours, I could find those slaves fast enough.

JUDGE: All right. You have my word that if you find my slaves, one of my fine horses will be yours. I'm staying at the inn, and you can find me there. But you have only until dawn to find them, as I have to leave town after sun-up. Come, Tandy. *(He bows to girls, then he and* MR. TANDY *exit, right.)*

HIRAM: What luck! I know this country inside and out. They must be nearby. They probably picked out a place that's right under our very noses.

PHOEBE: Surely you aren't planning to search for them, are you, Hiram?

HIRAM: My dear Phoebe, I am merely being a good citizen. If I stand to make a profit, that is my good fortune. I must get going. There aren't many daylight hours left.

ABE: Say, Hiram, I'll bet they're down by the river. They'd be hungry by now, and there are lots of fish to be caught.

HIRAM *(Snapping fingers):* You're right, Abe. I'll start there. I have to take this book inside first, though. *(He starts for steps, but* ABE *blocks his way.)*

ABE: No need, Hiram. I'm going back in. I'll take it for you.

HIRAM: Why, thanks. (*Hands book to* ABE) I want to get down to the river before it gets any darker.

ABE: Watch out for Lee. He gets a might riled if anyone disturbs his fishing.

HIRAM: He'll never know I'm around. (*He exits, left.*)

PHOEBE: I hope he doesn't find them.

ABE: Don't worry. Hiram isn't going to find the runaways.

MATILDA: Abe, why did you tell Hiram about the river?

ABE: If he had stayed here studying he might put me to shame at our spelldown tomorrow.

PHOEBE (*Laughing*): No one could ever beat you, Abe. We'll see you in school tomorrow. (*Turning*) Let's start for home, girls.

MATILDA: Do you want to walk with us, Abe?

ABE: I have to put Hiram's book away—you go on ahead. (*Girls exit, right.* ABE *looks down at book, then at schoolhouse, climbs steps and speaks loudly.*) I sure hate to go back inside. I could have sworn there were ghosts in there. (*A hand comes out through doorway and takes book.* ABE *walks down steps again and picks up his own book from the ground.*) This *Pilgrim's Progress* book is so interesting—all about a journey and the trouble a body can get into if he's not careful. Why, if I were on a trip right now, I'd be most wary about traveling at night. I'd start out after the sun comes up, when most people who have been out in the night would return to their beds, or be eating breakfast. I'd stay clear of main roads, too. (*He closes book and looks up*) Well—I'd better head for home. Ma will have supper waiting. (*Exits.* CALLIE *and* BIG JIM *come out of school.*)

BIG JIM: What a fine boy!

CALLIE: He knew we were hiding in the school, but never said one word to give us away. He could have had a reward, too. Why do you think he didn't tell on us?

BIG JIM: Don't know, Callie. Guess you can trust some people, after all.

CALLIE: He looked poor. His clothes were worn.

BIG JIM: Just the same, he is a gentleman at heart. I wish I knew his name.

CALLIE: I heard them call him Abe. Must be Abraham something.

BIG JIM *(Musing):* Abraham. That's a good name.

CALLIE: I'm never going to forget that boy. He's so tall and thin. I'll always remember it was Abraham who helped us slaves escape.

BIG JIM: I just wish he could help *all* our brothers and sisters escape. *(Pause)* We'd better get some rest while we can, Callie. Come. (*He takes her by the hand and turns to doorway.* CALLIE *looks offstage after* ABE *as lights begin to dim.* "The Battle Hymn of the Republic" *is played softly in background.*)

CALLIE: Our people are going to be free one day, Big Jim. I just know it. I feel it in my bones. (*She turns to go inside with* BIG JIM, *then turns once more toward audience.*) Abraham. That's a good strong name, Abraham. (*They go inside as* "The Battle Hymn of the Republic" *comes up loudly, perhaps with voices of choir. Curtain*)

THE END

PRODUCTION NOTES

ABE LINCOLN AND THE RUNAWAYS

Characters: 7 male; 4 female.

Playing Time: 20 minutes.

Costumes: Dark pants and shirts for Abe, Hiram, and Lee. Teacher wears suit with tie. Mr. Tandy and Judge Rollins, suits, hats and boots. Big Jim, pants, shirt, colorful bandana around neck. Callie, long dress, apron, bandana on head, and large earrings. Girls, long dresses, hair ribbons.

Properties: Two books; two riding crops; fish pole; burlap sack containing apples.

Setting: Indiana. Log cabin schoolhouse with steps and working door is center. Large window is on right side of house; bench stands near it. A wood pile with several logs of various sizes scattered around is in front of bench.

Lighting: At close of play lights dim, indicating dusk.

Music: "The Battle Hymn of the Republic."

The Abolition Flyer

by Louis Lerman

Characters

STORYTELLER
LEVI COFFIN
ARTHUR TAPPAN
WILLIAM LLOYD GARRISON $\left.\rule{0pt}{2.5em}\right\}$ *abolitionists*
HARRIET TUBMAN
JOHN HENRY
PEOPLE
PASSENGERS $\left.\rule{0pt}{1.2em}\right\}$ *extras*

AUTHOR'S NOTE

The Underground Railroad was the name given to the secret system of helping fugitive slaves from the South reach the free states and Canada before and during the Civil War. Beginning around 1804, fugitive slaves were taken, mostly at night, from station to station by "conductors" until they reached safety. Levi Coffin, whose home was an important station, became known as "president" of the Underground Railroad; other leaders of the movement included William Lloyd Garrison and Harriet Tubman. The legendary John Henry helped set the tracks through the Swannonoa tunnel in West Virginia, the longest and most difficult tunnel ever cut through a mountain. Many thousands of slaves—men, women, and children—rode the Underground Railroad to freedom.

STORYTELLER: In the days before the Civil War, they
used to say . . .

PEOPLE: The Underground Railroad—that's Quaker
Levi Coffin's road. He's president of it. Poor accom-
modations, but cheap traveling. The railroad runs
north from anywhere below the Mason Dixon line—
Florida, Georgia, Mississippi, Tennessee, the Car-
olinas. There was a time when it had a branch line into
the Kansas Territory, built especially for John Brown.
It went way up into Wendell Phillips's front parlor in
Boston, Massachusetts, then across the border into
Canada.

STORYTELLER: Now they tell this story:
Friend Levi Coffin
Was a railroad man
Ran the Abolition Flyer
To the promised land.

Had a locomotive engine
Nobody could see
But that Abolition Flyer
Made history

There never was
A train like that
A thousand miles
On a phantom track.

That train went riding,
Riding along
And the wheels were singing
A strange new song.

The people came
From miles around
To see that train,

To hear that song,
To ask if they could come along.

Levi's road had glory
His road had fame
For every slaver
Cursed his name.

But the road was poor
It lost money
Because Levi rode
All his passengers free!

So Levi gathered the Board of Directors at his house in Cincinnati. Among them were Frederick Douglass and Congressman Thaddeus Stevens and William Lloyd Garrison and Harriet Tubman and Arthur Tappan from New York. Levi opened the meeting with a prayer, then got down to business.

LEVI COFFIN: Friend Tappan, would thee be kind enough to give the financial report?

ARTHUR TAPPAN: Ladies and gentlemen, members of the board, Mr. Chairman . . . our assets to date are in the neighborhood of fifty thousand men, women, and children freed from slavery—including, I am proud to say, some members of our Board present.
We're in very sound condition
With a glorious tradition
For an apparition road
We're doing very, very well.
Only trouble is, we don't have any money. Not a cent.

COFFIN: Money or no money, Friend Tappan, we must expand. With the Fugitive Slave Law just passed by Congress, there will be three, four hundred thousand people waiting to travel north. It would be sinful not to take advantage of the business possibilities.

TAPPAN: You know as well as I do, Mr. Chairman, what shape the railroad is in. Coaches tumble down and engines stop. And the roadbed—well, no use even talking about that. Every slave-catcher in the United States seems to know that the stretch of road on the top of Smoky Mountain, between North Carolina and Tennessee, is bad. Can't do a thing until we get that fixed up. But where's the money going to come from?

COFFIN: The Lord will provide, Mr. Tappan.

WILLIAM LLOYD GARRISON: Is there anything *we* can do to help the Lord, Mr. Tappan?

TAPPAN: Well, we need labor. That's the big item.

COFFIN: Sister Harriet Tubman, do thee think we can get enough free labor down there to fix that stretch of road?

HARRIET TUBMAN: All we have to do is whisper we're coming, Friend Levi.

COFFIN: Friends, I propose that a small committee take a trip down and get a firsthand view of the situation.

STORYTELLER: That's the way it was decided. It was a nice, sunny day when they started out. The coaches and engine were cleaned up, oiled and greased. Harriet Tubman, with a big smile, sang out. (*Recording of train whistle and other sounds can be played in background.*)

TUBMAN:
All aboard for
Florida
Georgia
Mississippi
Tennessee

North and South
Carolina
and the Kansas-Nebraska Territory
Missouri
and all points South.

All aboard
The Abolition Flyer
Shovel the coal
Push the steam a little higher.
Wheels a'rolling
Rolling along
And the whistle blowing
That freedom song.

STORYTELLER: Engineer Coffin pulled the whistle cord three times. The steam started to hiss, the wheels started to roll, and with all the people on the platform yelling . . .

PEOPLE: Good luck! Good luck! Have a nice trip!

STORYTELLER: The train pulled out. The engine rolled along pretty well, except that every once in a while the firebox heated up and they had to stop and wait around until it cooled off. They could tell it was the South as soon as they hit it. Every time they stopped, even for a minute, there would be people around. Everyone seemed to know where the train was going, and how much a ticket cost. They just stood around, waiting for the train to start so they could get on board. At first, Harriet said:

TUBMAN: We'll pick you up on the way back. Get packed up and ready.

STORYTELLER: She told them where the station was. But there just wasn't room for all the people who wanted to go. After a while the train didn't stop. Couldn't stand the sight of people standing there, looking at them and asking questions without saying a word. There were times during the quiet part of the night when Harriet Tubman would sing to herself in a voice so low you could hardly make out the words:

TUBMAN:
My people came to me
And said:
Harriet Tubman, lift your head.

It's time, they said,
We lived like men
It's time we stood up straight again.

Tired of tears
And bitter bread
Time we tried to laugh instead.

I raised my head
And said to them
Brothers, it's a hard thing to be men.

This we know,
They said to me
But we will not live in slavery
We will not live in slavery.

STORYTELLER: Friend Levi sat in the cab, his eyes looking ahead as though staring into the future. Mr. Garrison shoveled coal without stopping, as though a fire built hot enough would burn out the curse of slavery. When they got to the end of the line, they overhauled the engine and checked the firebox. Then they started back North. Once in the plantation country, they stopped traveling during the day. At night they'd keep going, trying to move without noise. It was a hard job, with the old engine wheezing and the axles on the coaches creaking.

GARRISON: Slaveholders and patrollers would have to be stone deaf not to hear this train.

TUBMAN: It will be worse when we're loaded. We have reservations for a hundred times more passengers than we have room for.

COFFIN: Where are we going to put them all?

GARRISON: We'll make room for them even if we have to take the roofs off the coaches.

TUBMAN: We'll be getting to the station soon.

STORYTELLER: Engineer Levi let the engine coast along for a while. Harriet Tubman, standing by him, pulled the whistle cord. The sound spread all over the land, low and strong.

TUBMAN: Sounds as if it's calling the whole world.

STORYTELLER: They listened, and as the sound of the whistle died away, the echoes came clear, and the trees rustled with it, and the crickets fiddled the sound of it. And a stir and a whisper like a million people waiting on the station platform was heard.

GARRISON: Sounds as if the whole world has got word about our train.

TUBMAN: Word gets around. It always does . . .
   You can't keep the word from
      getting around
   When everybody listens for the word
      to sound
   And the word's in the sea, in the
      ground, in the air
   And the free wind's blowing it
      everywhere.

   People passing on the road say "Hello,
   Say, friend, did you hear the
      free wind blow?
   Say, friend, did you listen to

the wind and the sound?
Seemed to me it was saying:
  the word's going round!"

No, you can't keep the word from
  going round
When everybody listens for the
  word to sound
And the word's in the sea, in the
  ground, in the air
And the free wind's blowing it
  everywhere.

STORYTELLER: Friend Levi looked out, a big smile on his face, and watched the people climb into the coaches.

TUBMAN: The train's full, Levi. Not a bit of room anywhere. Passengers are standing in the aisles and sitting in the baggage racks. Let a few more on and there won't be room for you and Mr. Garrison.

STORYTELLER: She sings out . . .
All a-b-o-a-r-d
The Abolition Flyer
Shovel the coal
Push the steam up higher
Wheels a'rolling
Rolling along
And the whistle blowing
That freedom song.

PASSENGERS:
Got my ticket
On the Liberty Line
Leaving whip and chain behind.
Sing Hallelujah
Shout Amen
We get on slaves
And get off men.

STORYTELLER: Mr. Garrison shoveled coal and Friend Levi turned the throttle loose. The engine picked up steam and began to pound down the road a mile a minute. Everybody was smiling and feeling pretty good at the way that old engine was going. Suddenly, BANG—she stopped dead. Everybody stuck their heads out of the windows and yelled . . .

PASSENGERS: What's the trouble? Why are we stopping?

STORYTELLER: Far off they could hear the slavers' hound dogs baying. All the people—except the old ones and the children—got off the train, got behind it and pushed. They had a hard time getting her started, but they pushed her right up to Smoky Mountain. As soon as they got to the grade, she wouldn't move an inch. They'd push her ahead a bit, stop to catch their breath, and she'd slip right back.

GARRISON: Blast this blasted engine and this blasted mountain and the blasted slaveholders and their Congress and the Fugitive Slave Law and the Dred Scott Decision and Daniel Webster!

STORYTELLER: The sound of the baying hounds came closer and the children on the train began to cry.

GARRISON: No use. We need a lot more people than we have here to get this train over the mountain. It would take a majority of the people in the United States and the territories.

TUBMAN: Well, how about John Henry?

PASSENGERS:
Why, John Henry!
He's a man
Can do what a majority of people can.

TUBMAN: That's right. Get a majority of the people, and you can do pretty near anything.

PASSENGERS: And so can John Henry!

GARRISON: Get a majority of the people, and you can take this mountain and set it smack down in the middle of the Hall of Congress.

PASSENGERS: And so can John Henry!

COFFIN: Well, why don't we call him?

PASSENGERS (*Chanting in low tones at first, then increasing in volume*): J-o-h-n H-e-n-r-y . . . J-o-h-n H-e-n-r-y . . .

STORYTELLER: All of a sudden, everything was quiet, so quiet you could hear a noise like a big wind tearing the gound and the trees began to shake in the wind. The people looked up, and . . .
They saw a black man stand
As high as the mountain
With a hammer in his hand.

JOHN HENRY:
I'm John Henry.
They've been telling me
This road you're running
Rides my people free.

TUBMAN:
Oh, John Henry
I'm glad you could come.
We have to climb this mountain
Before the morning sun.

STORYTELLER: John Henry looked up and looked back. He saw the slavers behind him and the mountain ahead.

JOHN HENRY: It would take too long to climb the mountain with that old engine. And the roadbed's not much good. It's about time we got this stretch of road fixed. You all start pulling up that old spur on top of the mountain, and get the rails all piled up down here. We'll lay the rail underground . . .

Won't have trouble,
No grade to climb
Lose no passengers
On the Underground Line.

STORYTELLER: Then John Henry said to his hammer . . .

JOHN HENRY:

Lookit, old hammer
What you got to do:
Chop a hole through this mountain
Let liberty through.
Now, all you people
Better clear the track.
Once this hammer gets swinging
Mountain's liable to crack.

STORYTELLER: John Henry took one look around to see if everything was clear. He spit on his hands, hefted that hammer, and . . .

The earth it rolled
For ten miles under.
Mountain split
With a crack of thunder.
And it howled and it roared
And it stormed and it hailed
And the masters trembled
And the slave men quailed.
And people were saying . . .
What can that be?
Sounds like an earthquake—
Must be John Henry!

While John Henry was hammering through that mountain, the passengers were pounding out the roadbed and laying the rails. Fastest job of laying a roadbed you ever saw. And solid. That roadbed's better than a hundred years old now, but it's good as new. Fact is, it gets stronger every time somebody rides over it. The sun came up over the horizon, and the fog of slavery was lifted off the land. Harriet Tubman stood there waving to Friend Levi in the cab and Mr. Garrison shoveling coal. And the slave-catchers came into sight.

PASSENGERS: Get the engine started, Engineer Levi!

JOHN HENRY: Now, just take it easy. I'll push her to get you started.

STORYTELLER: John Henry took a running start, put both hands up against the back of the train, and pushed. That train shot down the grade into the tunnel as though shot from a cannon! The people on the observation platform shouted . . .

PASSENGERS: Much obliged, John Henry!

STORYTELLER: Their voices got fainter and fainter in the distance. Well, after that, of course, it was easy enough to expand that railroad. The Smoky Mountain stretch was always the best on the whole line. That's because President Levi Coffin got John Henry to be superintendent of the line!

THE END

Crispus Attucks

by Aileen Fisher

Born a slave—but who knows when?—
a fugitive from ruthless men,
Crispus Attucks made his way
to join a ship in Boston's bay.

He sailed the seas—who knows how long?—
this black man, young and tall and strong,
and then in a historic year*
it was his fate to reappear.

He walked with others of the crew
along the waterfront he knew,
and sensed a tension in the air:
"Why are these redcoats everywhere?"

"They're thrust upon us," townsfolk cried.
"We pay a tax that stings our pride.
We may not trade the way we please.
The English force us to our knees."

To Crispus Attucks, born a slave,
the colonists seemed less than brave.
And when the soldiers struck a lad,
he cried with all the voice he had:

---

*1770

"The way to get your freedom back
is not to grumble, but *attack*.
Come, follow. We've a stand to take
with rocks and clubs, for freedom's sake."

The redcoats flashed their bayonets
and shots rang out to still the threats.
Men fell before the rifle-burst,
and Crispus Attucks was the first . . .

The first to die in freedom's cause,
protesting England's stamp-tax laws,
the first to die for liberty,
before the war that made us free.

Daniel Hale Williams, Pioneer Surgeon

by Mary Satchell

Characters

DANIEL HALE WILLIAMS
ALICE WILLIAMS, *his wife*
ELLEN ANDERSON, *his foster mother*
DR. HENRY PALMER, *his mentor*
FRANK PEMBER, *doctor's apprentice*
CLARA BOYER   }   *student nurses*
EMMA REYNOLDS
LOUIS REYNOLDS, *her brother*
GRANT DAILEY, *an intern*

AUTHOR'S NOTE

Surgeon Daniel Hale Williams was born January 18, 1858, in Hollidaysburg, Pennsylvania. In 1883, he received an M.D. degree from Chicago Medical College, the medical division of Northwestern University, and eight years later, he organized Provident Hospital in Chicago. Provident's training school for nurses was the first for black women in the United States.

In 1893, Dr. Williams performed the world's first successful heart operation, and that same year, President Cleveland appointed him surgeon-in-chief of Freedmen's Hospital in Washington. During his career at Freedmen's Hospital, Dr. Williams married Alice D. Johnson. He later returned to the staff at Provident Hospital and remained in Chicago until his death in 1931.

SCENE 1

TIME: *Late spring, 1880.*

SETTING: *Dr. Henry Palmer's office. Desk and swivel chair left face door leading to patients' waiting room right; on desk are notepad, letter, pens, and pencils; chair is opposite desk; framed diploma hangs on wall over small medicine cabinet on table center; coat rack with man's coat draped over it stands beside door.*

AT RISE: DR. PALMER *sits writing at desk as* FRANK PEMBER *stands watching him.* DANIEL HALE WILLIAMS *unpacks box of bottles and arranges them in medicine cabinet.*

DR. PALMER: Frank, I'm very glad you've chosen to enroll at Chicago Medical College in the fall. That school has some of the finest teachers you'll find anywhere. (*He hands letter to* FRANK.)

FRANK: I'm fortunate to have a trust fund already set up for my education. And I appreciate your giving me such excellent references, Dr. Palmer.

DR. PALMER: We've all profited from the arrangement. After two years of study with me, you're more than ready to begin medical school. (*He turns in his chair toward* DANIEL.) And what have you decided about your future, Daniel? A fine apprentice like you should certainly go on from here.

DANIEL: Of course I'd like to go to medical school, too.

DR. PALMER: Have you talked with the Andersons about this?

DANIEL: Only once, a long time ago.

DR. PALMER: Then speak to Harry again when you go home. He thinks of you as a son, you know.

DANIEL (*Ceasing work and facing* DR. PALMER): The Andersons are not rich, Dr. Palmer. Harry already has enough problems to worry about without my adding to them.

DR. PALMER (*Kindly*): If my own son were not in college now, I'd lend you the money, Daniel.

DANIEL: It's most generous of you to say that, sir.

FRANK (*Getting coat from coat rack; putting it on*): What school would you select if you decide to go, Daniel?

DANIEL: My heart's been set on Chicago Medical.

FRANK: I hope you'll be able to go. I'd enjoy working with you there. Well, I have to be getting home. I'll mail your letter on my way, Dr. Palmer. (*Exits*)

DANIEL (*Approaching* DR. PALMER'S *desk*): Frank isn't the only one who had a trust fund. My grandfather set aside some money for me, but Mother had to use if after my father died.

DR. PALMER: Well, you've managed to come this far, and you've done better than some who had everything handed to them. (*Sound of bell ringing is heard.* DR. PALMER *looks at his watch.*) That must be Ellen Anderson. She has an eleven-thirty appointment.

DANIEL: I'll show her in. Harry's been trying to get her in for a checkup. (*Exits.* DR. PALMER *scribbles on a notepad until* ELLEN ANDERSON *enters.*)

DR. PALMER (*Genially*): Well, Ellen, you've finally come back to see me again after all this time! Please sit down.

ELLEN: Good morning, Henry. (*She sits.*) There's nothing wrong with me. I keep telling Harry that I don't need a doctor.

DR. PALMER (*Sternly*): You of all people should know how important it is to stay in touch with your doctor, Ellen. Have you already forgotten all you learned in nurse's training?

ELLEN *(Briskly):* Henry Palmer, you talk as though we were in school only yesterday. It's been fifteen years since I was a student nurse.

DR. PALMER *(Surprised):* Has it been that long? It seems such a short time since you decided to give up a promising career for a home and children.

ELLEN: So much has happened since then. But Henry, I really came to talk to you about Dan's future. He wants so much to become a doctor—a surgeon, in time—and I don't want to give up now. Harry agrees that we must help him.

DR. PALMER: I knew you'd feel that way.

ELLEN: I wanted to hear what you think about Dan's chances for success.

DR. PALMER: I had doubts when he first came, but that's all changed now. *(Firmly)* Daniel will become one of the great doctors of our time. Mark my words!

ELLEN *(Relieved):* Oh, I'm so glad you feel this way about him! Since Dan moved here, he's been like our son. And if he wants to be a doctor, Harry and I will help all we can. *(She rises.)*

DR. PALMER *(Springing from his chair, protesting):* Here now, where do you think you're going?

ELLEN: Henry, I have to go back to the children. I promise to make another appointment with you next week.

DR. PALMER *(Going with ELLEN to the door):* I will wait no longer than Thursday, and if you don't get in touch with me, I'll speak to Harry myself.

ELLEN: Next Thursday for sure, Henry. Goodbye. *(She exits, and a moment later DANIEL enters as DR. PAL-MER sits at his desk.)*

DANIEL *(Surprised):* Ellen's visit was so short. Is she all right?

DR. PALMER: Certainly.

DANIEL *(Relieved):* Good! I was worried for a second.

DR. PALMER: You shouldn't be worrying about anything today, Daniel. By the way, you may take the afternoon off and see about mailing a letter to Chicago Medical right away.

DANIEL *(Shocked):* An afternoon off! In two years that's never happened before!

DR. PALMER *(Dryly):* Mark my words, it will never happen again. Now, hurry on home. I think Ellen's got something important to tell you. (DR. PALMER *begins writing, and* DANIEL *rushes out the door as curtain closes.)*

* * * * *

SCENE 2

TIME: *1890.*

SETTING: *Office of Dr. Daniel Hale Williams, in Chicago. Desk, chairs and office door are arranged as in Scene 1. Diploma, medicine cabinet and coat rack are gone. Microscope is on top of desk.*

AT RISE: DR. DANIEL HALE WILLIAMS *is looking through microscope. A knock is heard. He rises and goes to door.*

DANIEL: Emma Reynolds, what brings you to my office on a cold night like this? (EMMA REYNOLDS *enters.)*

EMMA *(Taking off her coat):* Doctor Dan, I've come to ask your help. *(Upset)* I've tried everything!

DANIEL *(Kindly):* Hold on there, and sit down. Whatever the problem, it can't be that bad.

EMMA (*Sitting across from* DANIEL's *desk):* It *is* every

bit as bad as that, Doctor Dan. My hopes were so high when I came to live in Chicago with my brother. We thought there would be more opportunity here for black women in nursing, but it seems to me things are just the same as in Kansas.

DANIEL: I know you've been trying to get into nurses' training courses. No luck?

EMMA: No one will accept me.

DANIEL *(Sitting behind his desk):* You know, it's strange you should come to me just now with that problem. For almost a year I've been wanting to start my own hospital—a place where all people can come for medical care, no matter who they are, no matter what color their skin.

EMMA *(Surprised):* An interracial hospital? Who could dream of such a thing?

DANIEL: I've thought about it often.

EMMA *(Skeptically):* But, Doctor Dan, you'd need thousands of dollars to start a hospital, even a very small one! Where would the money come from?

DANIEL: From the people who live right here in Chicago. Surely they all want to help with such an important project.

EMMA: Why, that would be a dream hospital!

DANIEL: And your problem could be solved by the same dream.

EMMA: How?

DANIEL: If we were to start a hospital, we could easily set up a training program for nurses and interns.

EMMA *(Excitedly):* Why, now I understand! In your hospital, I could be accepted as a student nurse.

DANIEL *(Slowly and pointedly):* Yes, if you're qualified.

EMMA *(Laughing):* No need to remind me of that. *(De-*

termined) But I want this kind of chance too badly to miss out on it. I don't think I'd have any trouble qualifying for acceptance. When can I apply?

DANIEL *(Amused):* Wait a minute! You sound as if the hospital's open and ready for business.

EMMA: For a moment I *did* believe my career was a sure thing.

DANIEL *(Studying* EMMA's *face):* It *is* a sure thing.

EMMA: Doctor Dan, are you serious? Here it is 1890, and there's still no such place in the whole country.

DANIEL *(Determined):* I'm tired of watching helplessly while people are refused good hospital care even when they can well afford to pay. *(Another knock on door is heard.)*

EMMA: That's probably my brother. I told him to pick me up here this evening.

DANIEL *(Calling out):* Come in, the door's unlocked. (LOUIS REYNOLDS *enters.)*

LOUIS: So my sister was able to catch you before you left, Doctor Dan.

DANIEL: My house calls don't start for another half hour, Louis. How's that sprained shoulder coming along?

LOUIS: It's just about healed and gives me no trouble at all.

DANIEL: I'm glad to hear it!

LOUIS: Doctor Dan, is there anything you can do to help Emma? She's going to worry me to death if we don't get her into somebody's nursing school.

DANIEL: Emma and I have come up with a plan that will help a great number of women with the same ambition.

EMMA *(Enthusiastically):* Yes, Louis! Doctor Dan has solved the problem!

LOUIS: Thank heavens! What school do you think will accept Emma on your recommendation?

DANIEL: Well, she might have a chance to enroll in a new training school as soon as we can get it going. Probably in a year or so.

EMMA: I'd be willing to work and wait.

LOUIS (*Puzzled*): What are you two talking about?

EMMA (*Excitedly*): Oh, Louis, we're going to start our own hospital and nursing school right here in Chicago!

LOUIS: Doctor Dan, is she serious?

DANIEL: It's true. We're going to start a hospital. It will be small at first—no more than twelve beds—but it's sure to grow larger in time. Let's see—we'll call it the Provident Hospital and Nurses Training School.

LOUIS: But how will you get the money for such a place?

DANIEL (*Leaning across his desk*): Wait and see, Louis. Just you wait and see. (EMMA *smiles as* LOUIS *stares at* DANIEL *in amazement. Curtain*)

* * * * *

SCENE 3

TIME: *A few years later.*

SETTING: *Provident Hospital. At left is closed door of patient's hospital room. Scene may be played before the curtain.*

AT RISE: DANIEL *stands in front of door talking to* EMMA REYNOLDS *and* CLARA BOYER.

DANIEL: Well, I think we can finally relax now—Mr. Cornish is improving steadily. For the past week I've been holding my breath and praying. Just about everyone on the staff at Chicago Medical advised me not to attempt such a difficult operation.

EMMA: Who could really blame them? After all, Dr. Andrews said there are no records of any other successful heart operations.

CLARA *(Admiringly):* Few men would have the courage to open a man's chest and sew up a wound in his heart.

EMMA *(Proudly):* It was amazing! I would never have believed it could happen if I hadn't been there to see with my own eyes.

DANIEL: Somehow, I had every confidence that James Cornish would pull through.

CLARA: You know, Doctor Dan, I must admit that when you talked to me about joining Provident's nursing classes, I was reluctant to come to a hospital that had been in existence only a few years. *(Warmly)* Now, I'm sure that I couldn't have found a better place!

EMMA: Only six more months, Clara, and then you and I will be able to move out on our own!

DANIEL: Why, Miss Reynolds, I had no idea you were so eager to leave Provident, especially after all the work you did to help get it started.

EMMA: I've decided to go back home and use my nursing skills there.

DANIEL *(Kindly):* That news doesn't surprise me, Emma. Your decision is a good one. The more people we can serve, the better all our lives will become.

CLARA *(Glancing at watch):* It's time for me to make my rounds with Dr. Austin. I'll see you both this afternoon. *(Exits)*

EMMA *(Hesitantly):* Doctor Dan, there's a rumor you're think of leaving Provident Hospital soon, to take a job at a bigger hospital in Washington, D.C. Is it true?

DANIEL: So the grapevine is just as busy as ever. I can't

really say if it's true or not, Emma. I've been asked to apply for the job of surgeon-in-chief at Freedmen's Hospital, but I haven't made up my mind.

EMMA *(Distressed):* What would this hospital do without you? Look at all the achievements! A nursing school . . . hundreds of successful operations . . . how can you possibly leave?

DANIEL: Emma, try to understand what I just said to you and Clara Boyer about serving as many people as possible. At Freedmen's there are over two hundred beds, but the staff is inefficient and health care is poor.

EMMA *(Thoughtfully):* It seems to me that a national hospital set up after the Civil War to care for freed slaves should be better off than that. Perhaps you *should* take the job.

DANIEL: I've told myself the same thing, yet I hate to leave Provident. It's so much a part of me.

EMMA *(Respectfully):* Well, Doctor Dan, I'm only a student, but I have seen enough of your work to believe that you'd be the best man for the job.

DANIEL *(Gratefully):* Emma, you're always full of confidence. Your hometown will be lucky to have you back!

* * * * *

SCENE 4

TIME: *Early 1900's.*

SETTING: *Parlor in the Chicago home of Daniel and Alice Williams. Sofa and small table are center. Front door of house is right. At left is door leading to rest of house. Lamp, note, and book are on table.*

AT RISE: ALICE WILLIAMS *sits on sofa reading. Front*

door opens and DANIEL *enters, wearing overcoat and carrying a suitcase. He sets suitcase beside sofa.*

ALICE *(Putting down book and rising to embrace* DANIEL): What a surprise, dear! I wasn't expecting you for another two days.

DANIEL: Austin Curtis phoned me this morning saying I was needed at Provident on urgent matters. He didn't go into details. *(He pulls off his coat and throws it on sofa.)*

ALICE *(Worried):* Dan, you're working yourself too hard. Why do you care for everybody's health but your own? That hospital can surely get along without you for a week. They managed somehow during the years you spent at Freedmen's in Washington. I wish you'd get some rest!

DANIEL *(Affectionately):* Alice, you should write a book about the trials of a doctor's wife. *(He sprawls on sofa and stretches.)* I performed five operations a day at the Meharry College Clinic. There were young doctors visiting from all over the country—doctors who never had the chance to attend good medical schools or share ideas with experienced surgeons.

ALICE: I'm glad to hear that! *(Briskly)* Now, how about something to eat? Let me heat up some meat loaf and potatoes for you. *(She picks up coat and starts left.)*

DANIEL: That sounds delicious, Alice, but I had a sandwich on the train. I'm not at all hungry. (ALICE *stops and turns around.)*

ALICE *(Exasperated):* See, that's what I mean. You don't take proper care of yourself!

DANIEL *(Sitting up with his elbows on his knees and rubbing his temples):* Oh, I'm all right. (ALICE *joins him on sofa.)*

ALICE *(Warmly):* Tell me how it went.

DANIEL: Well, Dr. Purvis of Freedmen's was there, too. He said my nurses' training program is still growing. There were nearly one hundred graduates last term!

ALICE *(Warmly):* That's wonderful, dear. *(Suddenly)* Oh, while you were away, a doctor in Alabama called. He and his colleagues want your help with some serious cases, and asked if you would come down in a week or so. They offered to send you your fare.

DANIEL: Why, of course, I'll go.

ALICE: I knew you would. Your trips around the country must inspire so many doctors, Daniel.

DANIEL: It's the best way of reaching out to help. I've operated in log cabins, dining rooms, basements . . . Old Dr. Palmer and the Andersons helped me, and I intend to do the same for other people. *(Sound of telephone ringing is heard offstage.)* That may be Austin, calling to see if I'm here. (ALICE *exits, and there is a knock at right door.*) Everything is happening at once around here tonight! *(He opens door.)* Well, Grant Dailey! Come in. (GRANT DAILEY *enters.*)

GRANT: Hello, Doctor Dan. A lot of people will be glad to have you back. Booker T. Washington phoned the hospital twice since this morning.

DANIEL: From Tuskegee?

GRANT: Yes, Austin Curtis talked to him both times. (ALICE *rushes in.*)

ALICE: Dan, Austin says he has some important news for you. (DANIEL *exits left.*) Grant, do you know what happened?

GRANT: I'm not sure, Alice, but I think it's got something to do with Emmett Scott, Washington's private secretary. (ALICE *sets suitcase on sofa, then opens it to sort contents.* GRANT *paces until* DANIEL *returns after a few moments.*)

DANIEL: I have to catch the morning train to Alabama, Alice. Booker T. Washington's secretary is ill, and won't let anybody but me examine him.

ALICE *(Dismayed):* But, Dan, you got home only minutes ago!

DANIEL *(Sadly):* I know, Alice. But Emmett is my good friend, and I have to help him.

ALICE: I understand, dear. You'll need some clean clothes. I'll get another bag ready. *(Exits, carrying suitcase)*

GRANT: Here I was, coming to drop my troubles in your lap, and you're loaded down already.

DANIEL *(Kindly):* Sit down, Grant. There's always time to listen to you. What's the problem?

GRANT *(Sitting on sofa):* I have a patient at the hospital whose heart is badly damaged. I'm afraid it may be necessary to open his chest.

DANIEL: You should read the paper I wrote a few years after my first heart operation.

GRANT: I will, but perhaps first you can explain a few things to me. (ALICE *enters.* GRANT *rises.*)

DANIEL: Grant, excuse me just a moment. Alice, where in Alabama do those young doctors who called on me live? I wonder if it's anywhere near Tuskegee.

ALICE: I'm not sure. *(She takes note from table and gives it to* DANIEL.*)*

DANIEL *(Reading aloud):* Dr. John A. Kent, Union Springs.

GRANT: That's just south of Tuskegee Institute.

DANIEL *(Pleased):* I'll be able to pay them a visit after I treat Emmett Scott.

ALICE: At least you're sure to get good meals while you're with the Washingtons. They won't let you forget to eat! *(Exits)*

DANIEL *(Putting note in his pocket):* I wouldn't last long without Alice. Now, Grant. *(Sits on sofa)* Start from the beginning. Tell me every step you went through to examine your patient. My train doesn't leave until eight tomorrow morning, and I'll have a look at your patient before I say goodbye. *(They put their heads together as though starting a long discussion as curtains close.)*

THE END

PRODUCTION NOTES

DANIEL HALE WILLIAMS, PIONEER SURGEON

Characters: 5 male; 4 female.

Playing Time: 20 minutes.

Costumes: Period dress. Women wear long skirts and blouses. Ellen Anderson wears coat and small hat and carries purse in Scene 1, as does Emma Reynolds in Scene 2. Daniel and Frank wear trousers, long-sleeved shirts with garters above elbows, and small ties; Louis Reynolds wears overcoat in Scene 1. Daniel Williams wears white jacket; student nurses wear white uniforms in Scene 3. Daniel Williams wears overcoat and suit in Scene 4.

Properties: Box of glass bottles; suitcase packed with clothes.

Setting: Scene 1, Dr. Henry Palmer's office: Desk and swivel chair left face door leading to patients' waiting room right; on desk are notepad, letter, pens, and pencils; chair is opposite desk; framed diploma hangs on wall over small medicine cabinet on table center; coat rack with man's coat draped over it stands beside door. Scene 2, office of Dr. Daniel Hale Williams: Desk, chairs, and door are arranged as in Scene 1; diploma, medicine cabinet, and coat rack are gone; microscope is on desk. Scene 3, Provident Hospital: At left is closed door of patient's room. (Scene may be played before curtain.) Scene 4, parlor in home of Daniel and Alice Williams: Sofa and small table are center; on table are lamp, book, and note; door to rest of house is left; front door is right.

Lighting: No special effects.

Sound: Doorbell; telephone.

I Have a Dream

by Aileen Fisher

Characters

JEFF
SUSAN
GRANDFATHER
SAMUEL
OTHER AUDIENCE MEMBERS
M.C.
BUS DRIVER
MRS. ROSA PARKS
BUS PASSENGERS
POLICE OFFICER
MARTIN LUTHER KING
BLACK MEN AND WOMEN
DALTON
COREY
CHORUS, *6 or more male and female*
STAGEHANDS
MARCHERS
LOUDSPEAKER VOICE

BEFORE RISE: *Music of "We Shall Overcome" is played in background as several audience members enter from back of auditorium and go to front rows to take seats.* JEFF *and* SUSAN *enter, carrying on conversation.*

JEFF: Until we studied about Martin Luther King in school, I never realized what a difference he made to this country.

SUSAN *(Nodding):* He was a great man. I'm glad the school is honoring his birthday with this program. *(Looks around for seats)* Jeff, here are two good seats together. *(They sit.* GRANDFATHER *and* SAMUEL *enter at back of auditorium, start walking toward front.)*

SAMUEL: Where do you want to sit, Grandpa?

GRANDFATHER: Thanks to Martin Luther King, Samuel, we can sit any place we please. We black folks couldn't always do that.

SAMUEL: I know. We were considered second-class citizens, weren't we? When I hear you and Grandma talk about it, I wonder why it was like that.

GRANDFATHER: That's what Martin Luther King was always wondering—and asking. And he did something about it—something that changed the whole country. He reminded everyone that people in the United States should all have the same chance. That's what the Constitution says—"with liberty and justice for all."

SAMUEL *(Pointing to two seats):* Let's sit right here, Grandpa. *(Lights dim.)* The program's about to begin.

* * * * *

SETTING: *Stage is bare. M.C.'s stand is at one side of stage. At the other side are two rows of chairs, angled so that they face the audience. A large sign reading* RESERVED FOR WHITES *is placed near the chairs in front. Chairs at the back have sign reading* COLORED SECTION. *A single chair for Bus Driver is placed in front of the two rows. On the backdrop is a large picture of Martin Luther King. If available, slides of*

Martin Luther King and activities in which he was engaged may be flashed on the backdrop from a projector throughout the play.

AT RISE: *Spotlight goes up on M.C.'s stand. M.C. enters and addresses audience.*

M.C.: We are gathered here today to celebrate the birthday of a great American—Martin Luther King—who made a lasting impression on our history in his short life of 39 years. Actually, his career as a leader in the freedom movement didn't begin until he was 26 years old. Before that his life ran smoothly enough. He went to college, received a doctorate in theology, married, and became pastor of a Baptist church in Montgomery, Alabama. But on a December night in 1955, something happened that changed the direction of his life. Picture a crowded bus in the city of Montgomery, carrying passengers home after a busy day. (BUS DRIVER *enters, sits in single chair. BUS PASSENGERS enter and sit in chairs—white passengers in front section, blacks in back section. Spotlight goes up on chairs. BUS DRIVER pantomimes driving for a few moments, then stops. More PASSENGERS enter, pay fare to DRIVER, and take seats. MRS. ROSA PARKS, a black woman carrying heavy bags, enters, pays fare to DRIVER, then looks wearily at the chairs—mostly filled except for one in front section. She sits there.*)

PASSENGER (*Angrily; to* ROSA): You'll have to move to the back of the bus, lady. (ROSA *doesn't move.*) Can't you read? (*Points to* RESERVED FOR WHITES *sign*) These seats are for whites only. (DRIVER *looks around, gets up, and goes over to* ROSA.)

DRIVER: Lady, these seats are reserved. Go to the back of the bus where you belong. (ROSA *doesn't move or speak.*)

OTHER WHITE PASSENGERS *(Ad lib):* She won't move! Doesn't she know she can't sit in the front of the bus? *(Etc.)*

DRIVER *(Angrily):* All right, lady. You asked for it. *(Steps to center stage, calls off)* Officer! Officer, would you come here, please? (OFFICER *enters.)*

OFFICER: What seems to be the problem?

DRIVER *(Pointing to* ROSA): This lady is the problem. She won't move to the back of the bus.

OFFICER *(To* ROSA): You won't move, eh? *(Grabs her arm, pulls her out of chair)* Then you're under arrest. *(He drags* ROSA *off. Light goes out on chairs.* DRIVER *and* PASSENGERS *exit;* STAGEHANDS *remove chairs and signs. Spotlight goes up on* M.C.)

M.C.: For years black people in Alabama and other southern states had been treated as if they had no rights. If they complained, they were put in jail. White people made the rules, and black people were expected to follow them. But the arrest of Mrs. Parks aroused the black community in Montgomery to join together and do something. They turned to their pastor, Martin Luther King, for help. (MARTIN LUTHER KING, COREY, DALTON, *and several* BLACK MEN *and* WOMEN *enter, stand center stage.)*

1ST MAN: Reverend King, we have to fight against this injustice.

1ST WOMAN: What happened to Rosa Parks is a disgrace. We've all suffered enough from white people's laws.

COREY: Let's take action—now! Not next week or next year!

OTHERS *(Ad lib; angrily):* Yes, that's right! Let's fight! *(Etc.)*

KING *(Holding up hand for silence):* I agree the time has come to act. But we must do it peacefully, not with meanness and violence. Excited talk blocks common sense, and the only way for us to fight unjust laws is to unite against them. We have to fight injustice with words and nonviolent action instead of clubs or guns.

DALTON: Reverend King, I have an idea. What if we all boycott the buses—walk to our jobs and have our children walk to school, instead of riding in the back of the bus.

2ND WOMAN: But my job is five miles away! I can't walk that far twice a day!

KING: Dalton has a good idea. (*To* 2ND WOMAN) You could find a ride with someone who has a car. Anything but ride the bus. If we all unite to boycott the buses, then maybe the white men who make the laws will change those laws!

OTHERS (*Ad lib*): Maybe a boycott could work! Yes, let's try it. (*Etc.*)

KING: But always remember the boycott must be orderly, and peaceful. No threats, no fighting, no violence. We're not doing this out of hatred of the white men, but to make them see that our cause is just.

COREY: That's right, Reverend King. We're tired of being mistreated, tired of being kicked about. It's time to act, but in a peaceful way! When will the boycott start?

KING: Tomorrow morning! Let's spread the news to our brothers and sisters, and remember to impress upon them the importance of nonviolence. "He who lives by the sword shall perish by the sword." (KING *and others exit. Spotlight goes up on* M.C.)

M.C.: The very next day, December 5, 1955, the boycott began. Bus after bus clattered down the street with no black passengers. Bus after bus, day after day, for months—until finally, the law was changed and blacks could sit anywhere on a bus, not only in Montgomery, Alabama, but in other cities and states as well. (MARTIN LUTHER KING *enters and crosses to center stage. Spotlight comes up on him.*)

KING: At last the words of our Declaration of Independence are beginning to have some meaning! "We hold these truths to be self-evident—that all men are created equal; that they are endowed by their Creator with certain inalienable rights; that among these are life, liberty, and the pursuit of happiness."

M.C.: Other words, bold words, mighty words, were written into the preamble to the Constitution of the United States:

KING: "We the people of the United States, in order to form a more perfect Union, establish justice, insure domestic tranquillity, provide for the common defense, promote the general welfare, and secure the blessings of liberty to ourselves and our posterity. . . ." (KING *exits. Spot up on* M.C.)

M.C.: Martin Luther King's work for liberty had just begun. In many states, particularly in the South, white children and black children were not permitted to go to the same school; black children could not play in public parks. Many restaurants had signs in their windows: COLORED NOT WELCOME. One by one, Martin Luther King tackled the issues, driven on by his dreams of justice, and more and more black people looked to him for leadership. Meanwhile, Reverend King was put in jail again and again for his uncompromising stand on equality. His house was bombed. Still, his faith never wavered. (CHORUS *crosses backstage, singing first stanza of "We Shall Overcome."*)

CHORUS: We shall overcome
        We shall overcome

We shall overcome some day.
Oh, deep in my heart
I do believe
We shall overcome some day.

M.C.: Then came August, 1963, one hundred years after
Abraham Lincoln issued his Emancipation Proclama-
tion freeing the slaves. With the blessing of Martin
Luther King, more than 200,000 people, black and
white, took part in a "march for jobs and freedom" and
gathered at the Lincoln Memorial in Washington,
D.C., where Dr. King gave his famous "I Have a
Dream" speech. It was carried in newspapers all over
the country. (KING *enters, crosses center. Spotlight
goes up on him.*)

KING: I have a dream that my four little children will one
day live in a nation where they will not be judged by
the color of their skin but by the content of their
character.

I have a dream today.

I have a dream that one day the state of Alabama
will be transformed into a situation where little black
boys and black girls will be able to join hands with
little white boys and white girls and walk together as
sisters and brothers.

I have a dream today. . . .

And if America is to be a great nation this must
become true. So let freedom ring from the prodigious
hilltops of New Hampshire! . . .

Let freedom ring from every hill and mole hill of
Mississippi. From every mountainside, let freedom
ring.

When we let freedom ring, when we let it ring from
every village and every hamlet, from every state and
every city, we will be able to speed up that day when

all of God's children, black men and white men, Jews and Gentiles, Protestants and Catholics, will be able to join hands and sing that old Negro spiritual, "Free at last! Free at last! Thank God almighty, we are free at last!" *(Exits)*

M.C.: Martin Luther King's success in promoting non-violence as a solution to racial problems was recognized by the world in 1964, when he received the Nobel Peace Prize. He was only 35 years old, the youngest person ever to receive the prize. All over the world people watched on television as he accepted the award of $54,000. He donated it all to the civil rights movement. (KING *enters; spotlight goes up on him.*)

KING: On behalf of all men who love peace and brotherhood, I accept this award . . . with an abiding faith in America and an audacious faith in the future of mankind . . . and a profound recognition that non-violence is the answer to the crucial political and moral question of our time. Though 22 million of our black brothers and sisters in the United States are still fighting for full freedom and justice in nonviolent ways, I have faith that eventually they will achieve their goal, and that the long night of racial injustice will be over. I still believe that we shall overcome. *(Exits;* CHORUS *sings offstage.)*

CHORUS: We'll walk hand in hand
       We'll walk hand in hand
       We'll walk hand in hand some day.
       Oh, deep in my heart
       I do believe
       We'll walk hand in hand some day.

M.C.: The climax of Martin Luther King's career came in the spring of 1965, with the 54-mile march from Selma, Alabama, to Montgomery, the state's capital. It was a march to dramatize the "right to vote" problem. Although the 15th Amendment, ratified almost 100 years before the Selma march, gave blacks in this country the right to vote, blacks in some states still couldn't vote, because they were not allowed to register. This was an injustice that Martin Luther King was determined to fight. He faced bitter opposition in Alabama.

Hundreds of marchers, of every faith and race, started on the walk from Selma under a sweltering spring sun. But they had gone only a few blocks when they were met at a bridge by a living blockade of state troopers wearing helmets and swinging billy clubs. They carried canisters of tear gas. The marchers knelt down before the troopers, who pressed ahead swinging their clubs with abandon and spraying the air with gas. Dr. King saw that there was nothing to do but to retreat.

Two weeks later he tried again, this time leading 8,000 black and white supporters on the long march to the state capital. Meanwhile, a federal court order was issued to protect the marchers, and National Guard troops were on hand in case of trouble. Five days later the long march ended at the capitol building in Montgomery, where 25,000 people had gathered to welcome Reverend King and his fellow marchers. (MARTIN LUTHER KING *and* MARCHERS *enter, gather at center.*)

KING: We are on the move! And we are not about to go back. We will go on, with faith in nonviolent action, for our cause is humane and just. It will not take long, because the arm of the universe bends toward justice. . . .

MARCHERS *(Ad lib):* We will go on! *(Etc.)*

M.C.: As a champion of peace, Martin Luther King opposed the war in Vietnam. He spoke out against it with anxiety and sorrow.

KING: We must work for peace by peaceful means. War is madness, and this madness must cease. Those who love peace must organize as effectively as those who love war. (*Exits with* MARCHERS)

M.C.: For his outspoken views on this and many other national problems, Martin Luther King was continually in danger for his life. His family, too, suffered from threats, and several times the King home was bombed. In April, 1968, he went to Memphis to address striking sanitation workers. As usual his message was for peace, justice, and equality. No one was prepared for the violence that erupted. While Dr. King was speaking to a friend from the balcony of his motel, a shot rang out. Dr. King slumped to the floor. . . .

LOUDSPEAKER: Special news bulletin from Memphis, Tennessee! Martin Luther King has just been assassinated! Who the assassin is, no one knows at this point. We will supply more details as they come in. . . .

M.C.: Martin Luther King died just an hour after the shooting, a martyr to the cause of equality and peace. He was not yet forty years old. (*Music of "We Shall Overcome" is heard softly offstage.*) Yes, Martin Luther King had a dream, a dream for the future that will bring hope to the oppressed wherever they are, a dream to overcome injustice with fairness and equality. For as Reverend King said, the arm of the universe bends toward justice. (*Music of "We Shall Overcome" swells as curtain falls.*)

THE END

PRODUCTION NOTES

I HAVE A DREAM

Characters: 8 male; 2 female; 1 male or female for M.C.; male and female extras for all other characters.

Playing Time: 20 minutes.

Costumes: Jeff, Susan, Grandfather, Samuel, Other Audience Members and M.C. wear modern, everyday dress. All other characters wear clothes appropriate for the 1950's and early 1960's.

Properties: Shopping bags for Rosa Parks.

Setting: Stage is bare. M.C.'s stand is at one side of stage. At other side are two rows of chairs, angled so that they face the audience. Large sign reading RESERVED FOR WHITES is near chairs in front. Chairs at the back have sign reading COLORED SECTION. Single chair for Bus Driver is in front of the two rows. On the backdrop is a large picture of Martin Luther King. If available, slides of Martin Luther King and activities in which he was engaged may be flashed on backdrop from a projector throughout the play.

Lighting: Spotlights, as indicated.

Music: "We Shall Overcome."